PRACTICE
MAKES

Italian
Problem
Solver

Alessandra Visconti

Mc
Graw
Hill
Education

New York   Chicago   San Francisco   Athens   London   Madrid
Mexico City   Milan   New Delhi   Singapore   Sydney   Toronto

1   2   3   4   5   6   7   8   9   10   QVS/QVS   1   0   9   8   7   6   5   4   3

ISBN   978-0-07-179126-7
MHID   0-07-179126-4

e-ISBN   978-0-07-179127-4
e-MHID   0-07-179127-2

Library of Congress Control Number 2012947476

McGraw-Hill Education, the McGraw-Hill Education logo, Practice Makes Perfect, and related trade dress are trademarks or registered trademarks of McGraw-Hill Education and/or its affiliates in the United States and other countries and may not be used without written permission. All other trademarks are the property of their respective owners. McGraw-Hill Education is not associated with any product or vendor mentioned in this book.

McGraw-Hill Education products are available at special quantity discounts to use as premiums and sales promotions or for use in corporate training programs. To contact a representative, please visit the Contact Us pages at www.mhprofessional.com.

Also by Alessandra Visconti
Practice Makes Perfect: Basic Italian

This book is printed on acid-free paper.

Contents

Preface

Practice Makes Perfect: Italian Problem Solver is for intermediate learners who wish to overcome persistent and frequent errors. In this workbook, you will learn how to become more aware of when and why these errors occur. As your awareness increases, you will begin to identify gaps and errors and gradually build language proficiency and accuracy.

Each chapter is dedicated to a particular grammatical topic, so the book as a whole can be studied in any sequence. A general introduction to the topic is followed by a clear and extensive presentation, with examples and exercises that ensure comprehension of the material.

After checking your answers, highlighting errors (rather than erasing them), and making corrections in the margin, repetition of the same errors will diminish. Studies indicate that learners can make the same error numerous times, and that one set of problems must be corrected before moving on to the next. *Practice Makes Perfect: Italian Problem Solver* will accelerate this learning process and will give you a good foundation for future progress.

Practice Makes Perfect: Italian Problem Solver can be used as a self-teaching text or as a grammar review. The exercises have been designed to keep you focused and interested as you tackle and overcome each problem.

It is my hope that *Practice Makes Perfect: Italian Problem Solver* will be an engaging, practical, and systematic tool for those seeking to gain fluency and proficiency in Italian.

Spelling and pronunciation

Italian is a highly phonetic language, which means that, for the most part, words are written as they sound. Each letter of the alphabet corresponds to one sound only, with a few exceptions. Most Italian sounds also exist in the English language, although the articulation may be lightly more forward in Italian. With a little practice, it is not difficult for English speakers to acquire a good Italian accent. The sound of the flipped intervocallic **r** (between two vowels) corresponds to the English *t* sound in words like *daughter* or *better*. Once the single **r** has been learned, the double, or rolled **r** (as in the sound *brrrr!*) should not be too difficult.

The five vowels versus the seven vowel sounds

There are five vowels—**a**, **e**, **i**, **o**, **u**—but there are seven vowel sounds. The vowels **e** and **o** have two possible sounds each: open and closed. To most English speakers the difference is hardly noticeable. In some Italian regions speakers tend to close the **e**'s and **o**'s, while in others they tend to open them. These variations across the Italian language rarely interfere with communication and add regional color and character to the overall language.

  ♦ The closed **e** is pronounced with the tongue slightly raised, as in:

       pesca   *fishing*
       e   *and*

  ♦ The open **e** is pronounced with the tongue slightly lowered, as in:

       pesca   *peach*
       è   *is*

As you can see, these words have the same spelling but are pronounced differently. If the speaker does not pronounce the **e** exactly right, the context and the syntax can be counted on for clarification.

For example, if **gelato alla pesca** (*peach ice cream*) were pronounced with a closed **e**, the listener would not interpret it as *fishing ice cream*. The more logical meaning would automatically be understood.

Closed o and open o

The closed **o** is pronounced with the lips more rounded. The open **o** is pronounced with the lips more open and the jaw slightly lowered. The difference is subtle and

1

it will take a while before an English speaker will be able to distinguish between the two variations.

l'**o**ro (open **o**)   *gold*
l**o**ro (closed **o**)   *they*

In this example, the syntax and context would again clarify the meaning of the words.

c and g sounds

The pronunciation of the letters **c** and **g** are affected by the letters that immediately follow them. When followed by an **e** or **i**, they are soft, as in:

Lu**ci**ano
ciao   *hi / bye*
gelato   *ice cream*
gri**gio**   *grey*

Nota bene

The -**i** in Luciano and grigio is silent. Its only function is to soften the **c** and **g**.

When the letters **c** and **g** are followed by **a**, **o**, **u**, **h**, or any consonant, they sound like the **c** in *candy* and the **g** in *game*. This is called a **velar**, or hard **c** and **g**.

Mar**co**
spa**go**   *string*
spa**ghe**tti   *little strings* (literal)

Nota bene

In the word **spaghetti**, the **h** is added to keep the hard **g** sound.

There are some sounds that are made up of two letters but are pronounced as one combined sound. These include the following:

- **sc** followed by **i** or **e** is a soft *sh* sound, as in:

  scelta   *choice*
  scena   *scene*
  uscita   *exit*

- **sc** followed by any other letter is pronounced *sk*, as in:

  scatola   *box*
  scuola   *school*
  scherzo   *joke*

- **gn** is pronounced as one sound like the *ny* the word *canyon*:

  Sardegna   *Sardinia*
  giugno   *June*
  segno   *sign*

- **gl** when followed by **i** is pronounced like the double *l* in *million*:

  figlio   *son*
  moglie   *wife*
  luglio   *July*

*Read the following words aloud and indicate which words have a soft **c** or **g** sound.*

1. giusto

2. gusto

3. cento

4. calcio

5. giovane

6. ghiaccio

7. cena

8. Sicilia

9. chi

10. giugno

11. che

12. canto

13. c'è

14. laggiù

*Read the following words aloud and put them in the correct columns (**gn**, **sh**, **sk**, **gl**).*

giugno	miglio	sconto	prosciutto	bruschetta	luglio
aglio	scendere	ascoltare	sogno	sciare	montagna

GN AS IN **PRUGNA**	**SH** AS IN **SCIARPA**	**SK** AS IN **SCARPA**	**GL** AS IN **FIGLIO**
_____	_____	_____	_____
_____	_____	_____	_____
_____	_____	_____	_____
_____	_____	_____	_____

Stress and accents

Italian words are generally stressed on the second-to-last, or penultimate, syllable, regardless of how many syllables they have.

gelato   soprano   Alessandra   perpendicolare

The next most common stress pattern is on the third-to-last, or antepenultimate, syllable. These include the following:

- Most words ending in **-abile, -ibile** (*-ble* in English), **-evole, -ico**
- The third-person plural of most regular verbs in all tenses except for the future
- The superlatives ending in **-issimo**
- The ordinal numbers ending in **-esimo**
- Most infinitives ending in **-ere**

gondola	telefono	Napoli	Figaro	possibile	probabile
parlano	Ligure	responsabile	spendere	accettabile	

The next most common group is stressed on the fourth-to-last syllable and may be difficult, as this stress pattern is unusual in English. Many of these words, however, are actually verbs with one or two pronouns attached.

telefonami   diteglielo   mandamelo   salutameli

Finally, there are some words that are stressed on the final syllable. The **grave** (tilting downward) indicates an open e or o, and the **acuto** (tilting upward) indicates a closed **e** or **o**.

caffè   università   virtù   perché   parlò

There are also words that end in two vowels that require an accent when the stress is on the final vowel.

più   già

The written accent may be used to differentiate one-syllable words that are spelled identically but have different meanings. The most common of these are:

ACCENTED	NONACCENTED
dà (*gives*)	da (*from*)
dì (*day*)	di (*of*)
è (*is*)	e (*and*)
là (*there*)	la (*the*)
né (*neither, nor*)	ne (*of it*)
sé (*himself/herself*)	se (*if*)
sì (*yes*)	si (reflexive pronoun)

Some monosyllables, such as **tre**, **blu**, and **su**, are written with an accent when they are the last syllable of a compound word.

trentatré   milletré   tiramisù   Barbablù

ESERCIZIO
1·3

Read aloud the following words and indicate the accented syllables. If you're not sure where the accent falls, review the earlier explanation and examples.

1. perché

2. vendere

3. probabile

4. devono

5. amabile

6. città

7. diciannovesimo

8. bellissimo

9. artistico

10. leggere (*to read*)

Phrasal doubling

In most of Italy, phrasal doubling (**raddoppiamento sintattico**) is very common in native speech. It frequently occurs in opera, theater, and television. Learners with a good ear will pick it up naturally, as native speakers do. Phrasal doubling occurs when one word of a phrase causes the doubling of the initial consonant of the following word, even though it is written with a single consonant.

The words that trigger phrasal doubling include strong monosyllables (**a, che, chi, è, fra, ho, ma, più, sto, su,** among others) and all words accented on the final vowel (**caffè, perché, sarò, andò,** etc.). Weak monosyllables such as articles and reflexive or object pronouns do not cause phrasal doubling.

Here is a short list of common phrases that illustrate how phrasal doubling works. As you can see, each phrase in the first column consists of two words. In the second column the phrase is written as it is pronounced, with the accent on the stressed syllable.

WRITTEN	PRONOUNCED
a me	/ammè/
a presto	/apprèsto/
ho fame	/offàme/
sto male	/stommàle/
che fai	/cheffài/
già fatto	/giaffàtto/

Nota bene

Weak monosyllables (such as articles, unstressed personal and reflexive pronouns, **ci**, and **ne**) do *not* cause phrasal doubling.

ESERCIZIO

1·4

Read the following words aloud and indicate the stressed syllables in each. All of them have an irregular (not on the second to last) syllable stress.

1. gondola

2. chiamano

3. però

4. impossibile

5. caffè

6. studiano

7. preferiscono

8. Napoli

9. Taranto

10. Ligure

*Find the words with a soft **c** or **g**.*

1. gatto

2. spaghetti

3. generale

4. che

5. laghi

6. giunto

7. sgelo

8. bacche

9. bacio

10. celeste

Many word pairs have become one word as a result of phrasal doubling. Read the following words aloud, being careful to pronounce the double consonants.

1. frattanto

2. chissà

3. lassù

4. oddio

5. ovvero

6. soprattutto

Pronunciation tips for advanced learners

A less than perfect accent in a second language is generally not a problem, unless it interferes with communication. For those in certain professions, such as opera singers, translators, and language instructors, however, a near-native accent can be a valuable asset. With a little awareness and practice, a good accent is possible to acquire.

Once you have memorized the sounds of the alphabet and learned the few rules regarding the variants of **c** and **g**, **gli**, **gn**, the pronunciation of Italian is really not difficult for English speakers to learn. The most common errors made by intermediate or advanced speakers have more to do with syllable stress than with letter sounds. The difference in duration between stressed and weak syllables is much more salient in Italian. This is what creates the characteristic lilt with the stressed syllables lasting two to three times as long as the unstressed syllables. Another stumbling block is remembering the words which have the primary stress on the third- or fourth-to-last syllable, rather than the more typical penultimate syllable stress.

It helps to make a note of words with similar endings and syllable stress and to read them aloud, making sure to adequately lengthen the strong syllable. The stressed vowels in the following words have been highlighted. Each column follows a similar pattern. Read this list aloud, making sure to lengthen the vowel in the syllable you want to stress, which in all cases is the third-from-the-last. After you learn these examples, you will be more aware of others that follow the same pattern and can make a mental note of them as you hear them.

-olo/-ola	-fero	-ogo/-a	-ile/-ole	-ico/-ido/-omo
gondola	fiammifero	biologo	probabile	simpatico
secolo	pestifero	radiologo	facile	arido
sogliola	sonnifero	psicologo	piacevole	rammarico
diavolo	frigorifero	dialogo	possibile	economo

There are also many verb patterns with the third-to-last syllable stress. The first group includes the infinitive of most of the -**ere** conjugation verbs such as **prendere**, **leggere**, **vendere**, etc. There are a few -**ere** verbs that have a regular penultimate syllable stress (**bere**, **sedersi**, **vedere**, **avere**, and the three modals **dovere**, **potere**, and **volere**), but the majority of -**ere** verbs have the stress on the stem, or third-to-last syllable, and not on the infinitive ending. Read the following verbs, paying attention to stress the third-to-last syllable.

prendere   vendere   scendere   sospendere   credere

Another group are the regular verbs of the present indicative in the third-person plural. Remembering these two categories will save you from making one of the most frequent pronunciation errors. Most third-person regular and -**isc** verbs follow this stress pattern.

parlano	rivedono	dormono
chiamano	bevono	aprono
studiano	prendono	preferiscono
ritornano	trasmettono	interferiscono

Nota bene

More advanced learners should be aware that this pattern also occurs in the present subjunctive and the imperative of the third-person plural and applies to both regular and irregular verbs.

-are		-ere	-ire
parlino	stiano	abbiano	dicano
scusino	diano	siano	capiscano
vadano	facciano	debbano	vengano

Another set with this third-to-last syllable stress in the third-person plural includes certain -**are** verbs of four or more syllables. The infinitive form has the stress on the second-to-last syllable, like other -**are** verbs, but there is no rule for exactly where the stress will fall in the conjugated verb. The following examples have similar stress patterns, and as one gains familiarity, the correct stress placement will begin to occur automatically. Be aware that the same part of the verb stem is stressed in the singular and the third-person-plural forms. Make a mental note of the pattern, repeat each verb aloud a few times, and do this each time you encounter new verbs of this type.

INFINITIVE	FIRST- THROUGH THIRD-PERSON SINGULAR	THIRD-PERSON PLURAL
abitare	abito/i/a	abitano
telefonare	telefono/i/a	telefonano
indicare	indico/chi/ca	indicano
predicare	predico/chi/ca	predicano

ESERCIZIO

1·7

Choose the one word with the irregular accent in each sentence and read it aloud with the correct syllable stress. If you like, you can indicate the stressed syllable to remind you where the stress falls.

1. Dove abita tua sorella?

2. La lezione è molto difficile.

3. È probabile che arriverà tardi.

4. Non è semplice arrivare in quella piazza.

5. Preferisco il clima arido a quello piovoso.

6. Cantano molto bene quei ragazzi.

7. Se hai fame, guarda nel frigorifero.

8. Per secondo prendo la sogliola ai ferri.

9. Suo marito fa lo psicologo.

10. I miei amici mi telefonano stasera.

ESERCIZIO

1·8

Read each verb aloud and change it to the third-person plural, being careful to lengthen the stressed syllable in both forms.

1. abito

2. eserciti

3. paghi

4. indica

5. pratico

6. gioca

7. predichif

8. prende

9. leggi

10. evita

ESERCIZIO

1·9

The following words are all stressed on the third-to-last syllable. Read each word aloud carefully and place it in the appropriate column.

telefonano	timido	cardiologo	impossibile	devono
fossile	allergico	portatile	antipatico	economo
abitano	tornano	austriaco	ammettere	filosofo
dividere	fiammifero	esprimere	amabile	decidono
rispondere	analogo	disabile	riconoscere	ipocondriaco

THIRD-PERSON VERB	ENDS IN **-ILE**	ENDS IN **-OGO, -OLO/A, -OMO, -OFO, -ERO**	**-ERE** INFINITIVE	ENDS IN **-IACO**
_____	_____	_____	_____	_____
_____	_____	_____	_____	_____
_____	_____	_____	_____	_____
_____	_____	_____	_____	_____
_____	_____	_____	_____	_____
_____	_____	_____	_____	_____

Nouns, gender, and number

The English language distinguishes biological gender in humans and animals, but these words are not marked in any way for gender. For example, *woman* and *man*, *sister* and *brother* are different genders, but the final **-n** and **-r** are common to both. There are a few remnants of gender markers in English, such as **-or** for masculine nouns (*actor*) and -**ess** for feminine nouns (*actress*), but these endings are slowly becoming obsolete.

In Italian, the last letter of nouns and adjectives indicates gender (masculine and feminine) and number (singular and plural). Nouns ending in **-o** are generally masculine singular and nouns ending in **-a** are feminine singular. To form the plural, the final **-o** changes to an **-i** in the masculine form, and the final **-a** changes to an **-e** in the feminine form.

MASCULINE NOUNS	FEMININE NOUNS
zi**o** → zi**i**	zi**a** → zi**e**
fratell**o** → fratell**i**	sorell**a** → sorell**e**
nonn**o** → nonn**i**	nonn**a** → nonn**e**
gatt**o** → gatt**i**	donn**a** → donn**e**

These nouns all refer to animate beings of the masculine and feminine genders. But nouns that refer to inanimate things or ideas also have gender in Italian, and this gender has nothing at all to do with biological gender. In fact the gender of some nouns varies within romance languages. The words for *sea* and *flower*, for example, are masculine in Italian (**il mare, il fiore**) but feminine in French.

Categories of masculine and feminine words

There are some categories of words that tend to be masculine.

- Trees

il melo	l'arancio	il pero
apple tree	*orange tree*	*pear tree*

Exceptions:

la quercia	la palma
oak tree	*palm tree*

- Metals, minerals, and elements

l'oro	l'argento	l'ossigeno
gold	*silver*	*oxygen*

◆ Mountains, seas, rivers, and lakes

il Monte Bianco	l'Arno	il Mediterraneo
Mont Blanc	*Arno river*	*Mediterranean sea*

The following categories are generally feminine.

◆ Fruits

la mela	l'arancia	la pera
apple	*orange*	*pear*

Exceptions:

il limone	il fico	il pompelmo
lemon	*fig*	*grapefruit*

◆ Arts and sciences

la fisica	la chimica	la matematica	la musica
physics	*chemistry*	*mathematics*	*music*

◆ Continents, countries, regions, and cities

l'Europa	l'Italia	la Toscana	la Roma antica
Europe	*Italy*	*Tuscany*	*ancient Rome*

Most nouns ending in **-tà** and **-tù** are feminine.

l'età	la città	l'università	la gioventù
age	*city*	*university*	*youth*

Those ending in **-i**, **-ione**, **-ice**, **-ie**, and **-ine** and are generally feminine.

la stazione	la scrittrice	la specie	l'origine
station	*writer*	*species*	*origin*

Nouns ending in **-i** in the singular (usually cognates of Greek origin that end in *-is* in English) are feminine and do not change spelling in the plural.

l'analisi	la crisi	la tesi	la metropoli	la diagnosi
analysis	*crisis*	*thesis*	*metropolis*	*diagnosis*

Nouns that have been abbreviated keep the gender of the original.

la fo**to**	*from* la fotograf**ia**
la bic**i**	*from* la biciclet**ta**
il cinem**a**	*from* il cinematograf**o**
la mo**to**	*from* la motociclet**ta**
la radi**o**	*from* la radiotrasmittente

Nouns of foreign origin ending in consonants are generally masculine.

lo sport	il bar	il tennis	il computer

Many words of Greek origin ending in **-a** are masculine.

il problema	il sistema	il melodramma	il poema
problem	*system*	*melodrama*	*poem*

Nouns ending in -e can be either masculine or feminine, but those ending in -one, -ore, -ale, and -ile are generally masculine (except for **automobile**).

il sapone	il colore	il giornale	il campanile
soap	*color*	*newspaper*	*bell tower*

Nota bene

Many nouns from Greek or Latin have similar stems in English and are called *cognates*. Recognizing cognates will increase your vocabulary by hundreds of words! With a little practice you can recognize them instantly and use them to form other related words. For example, most English nouns ending in *-tion* are cognates and are feminine.

nazione	situazione	illustrazione
nation	*situation*	*illustration*

Other cognates include words in Italian ending in -**or** or -**er**, which are usually masculine.

dottore	trattore	attore	promotore
doctor	*tractor*	*actor*	*promotor*

ESERCIZIO
2·1

Provide the definite article for each of the following singular nouns.

1. _____ giornale
2. _____ lezione
3. _____ sport
4. _____ solitudine
5. _____ stazione
6. _____ dilemma
7. _____ frigo
8. _____ portale
9. _____ crisi
10. _____ virtù

Masculine and feminine suffixes

Some nouns that refer to humans and animals change gender simply by changing the endings -o or -e to an –a: -e / -ore → -ice / -essa. Others, however, add a suffix, as shown in the table on the next page. Notice how the nouns that have a double **tt** in the masculine favor the suffix -**rice** in the feminine.

MASCULINE	FEMININE	
principe	principe**ssa**	*prince/princess*
professore	professor**essa**	*professor*
studente	studen**tessa**	*student*
scrittore	scritt**rice**	*writer*
direttore	dirett**rice**	*director*
attore	att**rice**	*actor/actress*

Some nouns have slightly different masculine and feminine forms.

dio	*god*	dea	*goddess*
re	*king*	regina	*queen*
cane	*dog*	cagna	*female dog*
gallo	*rooster*	gallina	*hen*

Other nouns have different roots.

padre	*father*	madre	*mother*
fratello	*brother*	sorella	*sister*
marito	*husband*	moglie	*wife*
genero	*son-in-law*	nuora	*daughter-in-law*
maschio	*male*	femmina	*female*
uomo	*man*	donna	*woman*

Finally, there is a group of nouns that has only one form for both masculine and feminine. The gender for these nouns will be marked only by an article, adjective, or context.

♦ **-e**

il nipote	la nipote	*nephew / niece, grandson / granddaughter*
il parente	la parente	*relative*

♦ **-ista**

il pianista	la pianista	*pianist*
l'artista	l'artista	*artist*
il socialista	la socialista	*socialist*

♦ **-a**

il collega	la collega	*colleague*
l'atleta	l'atleta	*athlete*
il maratoneta	la maratoneta	*roadrunner*

♦ **-ante** or **-ente** (These nouns are generally derived from verbs.)

il cantante	la cantante	*singer*
l'amante	l'amante	*lover*
l'insegnante	l'insegnante	*teacher*
il presidente	la presidente	*president*
il dirigente	la dirigente	*executive*

The following sentences are examples of how a noun's gender is revealed at the end of the sentence by the adjective. To reduce ambiguity, native speakers may include a proper name or a relative clause that will clarify the gender earlier on in the sentence.

L'insegnante di matematica è simpatic**a**.	*The math teacher is nice.*
L'insegnante di storia è altissim**o**.	*The history teacher is very tall.*

Nota bene

As we have seen, nouns that refer to living things often change their endings from -o to -a to indicate gender. Watch out for nouns that seem to have a masculine and feminine form but are actually unrelated words of totally different meaning. Associating these words with an adjective may help you connect gender with meaning; for example, **la porta aperta** vs. **il porto marino**.

il caso	*case*	la casa	*house*
il colpo	*hit*	la colpa	*fault*
il filo	*thread*	la fila	*line, cue*
il modo	*way*	la moda	*fashion*
l'oro	*gold*	l'ora	*hour*
il porto	*seaport*	la porta	*door*

Professions

Although many professions are open to all genders, some professions still lack a feminine form. In these cases, the article is masculine and the gender can be understood from the context: **il soprano Maria Callas, il ministro Rosy Bindi**. As more and more female ministers, lawyers, architects, and engineers emerge, these words gain a feminine form, and it is not so uncommon to see written or to hear **la ministra, l'avvocatessa,** or **l'architetta**. In prescriptive grammar, there is a preference for the following nouns to remain masculine regardless of gender.

l'avvocato	*lawyer*	il soprano	*soprano*
il medico	*physician*	il mezzosoprano	*mezzo-soprano*
l'ingegnere	*engineer*	il contralto	*alto*
l'architetto	*architect*	il maestro	*teacher*

In professions ending in **-ente**, which are derived from verbs, the article changes according to the gender.

il/la presidente	*the president*
il/la conoscente	*the acquaintance*
il/la sovrintendente	*the superintendent*

ESERCIZIO

2·2

Indicate the missing nouns.

MASCULINE	FEMININE
signore	_____
_____	dottoressa
padre	_____
_____	professoressa
studente	_____
_____	scrittrice

nipote _____

_____ sorella

uomo _____

Add the definite article to the following words, and then match them with their English equivalents.

1. _____ gallina   a. *row*

2. _____ porto   b. *engineer*

3. _____ casa   c. *hen*

4. _____ nipote   d. *nephew/niece*

5. _____ filo   e. *port*

6. _____ colpa   f. *home*

7. _____ ingegnere   g. *fashion*

8. _____ moda   h. *thread*

9. _____ fila   i. *fault*

10. _____ medico   j. *physician*

Change the gender of the following articles and nouns. **Attenzione!** Some nouns are invariable.

1. la nipote _____

2. la scrittrice _____

3. il presidente _____

4. la collega _____

5. l'uomo _____

6. la moglie _____

7. la dottoressa _____

8. il dio _____

9. la nuora _____

10. l'insegnante _____

Number: Singular or plural

Nouns in Italian change their final letters to indicate number (singular or plural). Most nouns follow this simple formula:

- Masculine nouns ending in **-o** → **-i**

  ragazzo → ragazzi

- Feminine nouns ending in **-a** → **-e**

  ragazza → ragazze

- All nouns ending in **-e** (regardless of gender) → **-i**

  (*m.*) signore → signori
  (*f.*) nipote → nipoti

Some nouns are invariable:

- Nouns that end in a consonant (usually foreign words)
- Monosyllables (**il re → i re**)
- Feminine nouns ending in **-i** (**la tesi → le tesi**)
- Feminine nouns ending in **-ie** (**la serie → le serie**)
- Nouns ending in an accented vowel (**il caffè → i caffè**, **la città → le città**)

Nouns that end **-o** or **-e** form the plural by changing the **-o** or **-e** to an **-i**, regardless of gender. When two **-i**'s result, one is dropped unless it is accented.

padre → padri   madre → madri   moglie → mogli   zio → zii

Feminine nouns that end in **-a** form the plural by changing the **-a** to an **-e**.

donna → donne   mamma → mamme

However, feminine nouns ending in **-ca** or **-ga** add an **h** in the plural to maintain the hard **c** or **g** sound. (See **c** and **g** sounds in Chapter 1.)

amica → amiche   biologa → biologhe

Feminine nouns ending in **-ccia** and **-ggia** with an unaccented **i** drop the **i** in the plural, as it is no longer needed to soften the **c** or **g**.

focaccia → focacce   pioggia → piogge

However, if the **-cia** or **-gia** ending is preceded by a vowel, the softening **i** is retained.

camicia → camicie   valigia → valigie

Masculine nouns ending in **-co** or **-go** (with very few exceptions) add an **h** to keep the hard **c** or **g** sound in the plural.

lago → laghi   albergo → alberghi   parco → parchi   affresco → affreschi

Exception:

amico → amici   greco → greci

When accented on the third-to-last syllable, most masculine nouns do not add an **h** in the plural and the **c** or **g** softens.

sindaco → sindaci   biologo → biologi

Masculine nouns ending in a monosyllabic **-io** form the plural with a single **-i**.

negozio → negozi   stadio → stadi   figlio → figli

When the **-i** of the diphthong is accented, both **i**'s are retained in the plural.

zio → zii

ESERCIZIO
2·5

Indicate which column each singular noun belongs to and add the plural forms.

stadio   università   sport   parco   medico

camicia   film   focaccia   zio   tesi

MASCULINE SINGULAR	MASCULINE PLURAL	FEMININE SINGULAR	FEMININE PLURAL
_____	_____	_____	_____
_____	_____	_____	_____
_____	_____	_____	_____
_____	_____	_____	_____
_____	_____	_____	_____

Articles

The definite (*the*) or indefinite article (*a*) precedes the noun and indicates the gender (masculine or feminine) and the number (singular or plural) of the noun. The definite article is used with known and specific nouns (*the book*), while the indefinite article is used with unknown and unspecific nouns (*a book*).

The indefinite article

The indefinite article (**un, uno, un', una, un'**) varies depending on the gender and first letter of the word that follows. It is used with singular nouns that are unspecific or unknown, and corresponds to *a/an* or *one* in English.

- With masculine nouns that begin with most consonants or a vowel, **un** is used:

  un libro   *a book*   un amico   *a friend*

- With masculine nouns starting with a **z**, **ps**, or **gn**, **s** + consonant, **y**, or **io**, **uno** is used to create a smoother sound:

  uno zio   *uncle*   uno psicologo   *psychologist*   uno gnocco   *type of pasta*
  uno studente   uno yoghurt

- With feminine nouns that begin with all consonants, **una** is used:

  una musica   una studentessa   *female student*

- With feminine nouns that begin with a vowel, **un'** is used:

  un'aria   un'automobile

Nota bene

The apostrophe is used only with the feminine article to substitute for the dropped final **-a**. The pronunciation of **un** and **un'** is identical. When an adjective precedes the noun, the first letter of the adjective will determine the form of **un** to be used.

  un'amica   **una** bella amica   *a pretty friend*
  un libro   **uno** strano libro   *a strange book*

Change the following nouns to the singular, and then add the indefinite article.

1. stadi _____

2. insalate _____

3. psicologi _____

4. automobili _____

5. città _____

6. stazioni _____

7. mani _____

8. serie _____

9. alberghi _____

10. tedeschi _____

The definite article

The definite article (**il**, **lo**, **l'**, **la**, **i**, **gli**, **le**) varies according to the gender and number of the noun, and the first letter of the word that follows. It has four singular and three plural forms.

STARTS WITH	MASCULINE SINGULAR	MASCULINE PLURAL
a consonant **s** + consonant, **z**, **x**, **gn**, **ps**, **y**, or **io**	il cantante (*singer*), il violino lo studente, lo zio (*uncle*), lo yoghurt, lo iodio (*iodine*)	i cantanti, i violini gli spaghetti, gli zii, gli gnocchi, gli psicologi, gli Stati Uniti
a vowel	l'amico (*friend*), l'albero (*tree*)	gli amici, gli alberi

STARTS WITH	FEMININE SINGULAR	FEMININE PLURAL
a consonant	la sorella (*sister*), la matematica	le sorelle, le studentesse
a vowel	l'amica, l'America	le amiche, le Americhe

The definite article is used more frequently in Italian than in English. Following are some examples that demonstrate when the definite article is needed in Italian but not in English.

- With abstract nouns

la paura	la sete	il bisogno
fear	*thirst*	*need*

- With nouns that indicate matter or the elements

il legno	l'acqua	l'aria	il ferro
wood	*water*	*air*	*iron*

- With nouns that indicate a category, a species, or a group

la vita	l'uomo	i fiori	i pomodori	i violinisti
life	*mankind*	*flowers*	*tomatoes*	*violinists*

Nota bene

Since in English the definite article may be omitted, it is helpful to repeat these nouns and their articles in Italian as one inseparable unit.

Proverbi

| L'abito non fa **il** monaco. | *The habit does not make the monk.* |
| **La** notte porta consiglio. | *Night brings (good) advice.* |

Articles and proper names

The definite article is used before names of continents, countries, large islands, lakes, mountains, rivers, but not with cities. (Exceptions include Israel and Cuba, where the article is dropped.)

l'Italia gli Stati Uniti il Canada la Sardegna l'Europa gli Appennini

The definite article often precedes the last names of famous men but is optional. When using both first and last names, no article is used.

il Petrarca   Petrarca   Francesco Petrarca

However, with women's last names the definite article must be used.

la Callas (*or* Maria Callas)   **la** Loren (*or* Sophia Loren)   **la** Morante (*or* Elsa Morante)

When referring to a family or a married couple, the family name remains unaltered and the plural definite article is used.

i Simpson   **i** Medici   **gli** Sforza

When using titles such as **signora**, **signore**, **dottore**, **avvocato**, and **professore/essa**, the definite article is used when referring to a third person.

la signora Rossi   **la** professoressa Mancini

The article is omitted, however, when speaking directly to the person.

Buongiorno, avvocato Agnelli!   Buonasera, dottor Rossi.

Nota bene

Titles in Italian are not capitalized as they are in English. Neither are days of the week, months, and adjectives of nationality.

Il professor Orlando, che insegna martedì e giovedì, è siciliano.
Professor Orlando, who teaches on Tuesdays and Thursdays, is Sicilian.

Cities do not take a definite article, unless it is part of the name. In this case, the article is capitalized.

L'Aquila   **La** Spezia   **Il** Cairo

When referring to literary, artistic, or musical works, the definite article is used and is lower case.

la *Divina Commedia*   **le** *Nozze di Figaro*   *l'Aida*

The definite article is generally used before possessive adjectives.

il mio amico   la loro casa   i tuoi vestiti
my friend   *their home*   *your clothes*

The adjectives **tutto** (*all*) and **ambedue** (*both*) are followed by the definite article.

tutto **il** giorno   ambedue **le** amiche   tutti e quattro **gli** studenti

The definite article is used with seasons, days of the week, parts of the day, and specific hours of the day.

Amo **la** primavera.   **La** mattina mi alzo presto.   Sono **le** otto.
I love spring.   *I wake up early in the morning.*   *It is 8 o'clock.*

Lavoro sempre **la** domenica.
I always work on Sundays.

In certain prepositional phrases the definite article is omitted. These set phrases are better learned as one unit so that the omission of the article becomes automatic.

a casa   a scuola   a teatro   a letto
in campagna   in città   in montagna   in giardino   in spiaggia

However, there are some exceptions:

al mare (See combined prepositions, p. 100.)

With the verb **parlare** + a language, the article may be omitted, while with other verbs followed by a language such as **studiare**, **ricordare**, **amare**, etc. using the article is preferred.

Studio **l'**italiano da un mese.   *I have been studying Italian for a month.*
Si parla catalano in Sardegna?   *Is Catalan spoken in Sardinia?*

ESERCIZIO
3·2

Add the definite article to the following phrases where necessary.

1. _____ signora Bianchi

2. _____ Maria Callas

3. _____ scienze politiche

4. _____ Stati Uniti

5. _____ Canada (*m.*)

6. _____ New York

7. _____ autunno

8. _____ otto di mattina

9. _____ Alpi

10. _____ Cuba

Add definite the articles to the following singular nouns, and then change them to the plural form.

1. _____ sport _____

2. _____ aria _____

3. _____ tesi (f.) _____

4. _____ film _____

5. _____ foto _____

6. _____ auto _____

7. _____ estate (f.) _____

8. _____ papà _____

9. _____ psichiatra _____

10. _____ parentesi (f.) _____

Adjectives

Adjectives have a close relationship to the nouns they modify. They generally appear close to that noun, usually following it. They agree with the noun in gender and number. This is often problematic for speakers of English, where adjective-noun agreement does not occur. For example, in English we say:

> *Those paintings are very beautiful.*

In English, the adjectives *those* and *beautiful* are invariable. Here is the same sentence in Italian:

> Quest**i dipinti** sono molto bell**i**.

Notice the words in the sentence that agree with the subject (**dipinti**) by changing their last letter to **-i**. The adjectives have changed their endings to agree with the noun, which is masculine plural. This is known as adjective-noun agreement.

Adjectives describe the quality of a noun (color, shape, size, psychological, physical and moral characteristics, etc.) as well as the quantity, nationality, possession, and so on.

There are four types of adjectives in Italian: four-form adjectives (the most frequent), two-form adjectives, three-form adjectives, and one-form, or invariable adjectives (the least frequent).

How important is it to make the agreement between the noun and the adjective? Mismatching gender does not usually interfere with communication, but one of the distinctions between a beginner and an intermediate or advanced learner lies in the ability to make the agreement automatically and consistently. Every time you use the wrong form, you reinforce it in your memory, and chances are you will make the same error again. If you practice the more difficult adjectives (the one-, two- and three-form adjectives) and repeat the the noun and adjectives as one chunk, your memory of the sounds will help you when the time comes to use them.

Four-form adjectives

There are several different types of adjectives in Italian, and they are distinguished by the base form of the masculine singular and by the way number and gender agreement is formed. The most frequently encountered is the four-form adjective. When consulting the dictionary, you will find the base form of the adjective, always the masculine singular form, which ends in **-o**.

italian**o**   ross**o**   larg**o**   poc**o**

The four-form adjective agrees with the noun in gender and in number by changing its ending to:

- **-a** for feminine singular

    italian**a**   ross**a**   larg**a**   poc**a**

- **-i** for masculine plural

    italian**i**   ross**i**   largh**i**   poch**i**

- **-e** for feminine plural

    italian**e**   ross**e**   largh**e**   poch**e**

In **poco** and **largo**, notice how in the plural an **-h** is added to keep the hard sound of the letters **c** and **g**.

ESERCIZIO
4·1

Change the following nouns and adjectives from the singular to the plural.

1. libro giallo _____

2. studente universitario _____

3. piazza romana _____

4. buona regola _____

5. seta leggera _____

6. vestito chiaro _____

7. pizzeria antica _____

8. quadro famoso _____

9. cara amica _____

10. strada silenziosa _____

Two-form adjectives

The second most common type of adjective is the two-form adjective, which ends in an **-e** in both the feminine and masculine singular.

    elegant**e**   verd**e**   frances**e**   possibil**e**

In the plural, both feminine and masculine forms end in **-i**.

SINGULAR	PLURAL
uno studente francese	due studenti francesi
una studentessa francese	due studentesse francesi

Nota bene

As you can see, the masculine and feminine forms are identical, which means that they are not marked for gender, but only for number. There are always other factors in a sentence that will be marked for gender, such as the nouns, articles, other adjectives, and of course, context. In the following sentence, the words **verdi** and **eleganti** could be either gender, but **quelle** and **scarpe** both indicate a feminine subject.

Quelle scarpe verd**i** sono elegant**i**.
Those green shoes are elegant.

ESERCIZIO

4·2

Change the following phrases from the plural to the singular. All the adjectives are two-form.

1. ragazze intelligenti _____

2. libri interessanti _____

3. città affascinanti _____

4. attrici francesi _____

5. sport internazionali _____

6. domande difficili _____

7. bambini vivaci _____

8. vestiti eleganti _____

9. lezioni importanti _____

10. film francesi _____

Three-form adjectives

The three-form adjectives often correspond to English cognates that end in **-ist**, such as *optimist*, *feminist*, *violinist*, etc. Three-form adjectives have one form in the singular that ends in **-a**, and two forms in the plural.

SINGULAR (**-ISTA**)	PLURAL (**-ISTI** MASCULINE/**-ISTE** FEMININE)
un amico ottimist**a** (*m.*)	due amici ottimist**i** (*m.*)
un'amica ottimist**a** (*f.*)	due amiche ottimist**e** (*f.*)

Although these two-form and three-form singular adjectives do not always indicate gender, other adjectives and articles surrounding the nouns, as well as context, will usually clarify it.

One-form, or invariable, adjectives

One-form, or invariable, adjectives include foreign words and the names of colors.

scarpe **blu**	fiori **viola**	ristorante **chic**
blue shoes	*purple flowers*	*chic restaurant*

Any time adjectives are combined with a noun or another adjective, they become one-form, or invariable.

guanti verd**e** bottiglia	scarpe ross**o** fiamma	fiore **rosa** pallido
dark green gloves	*bright red shoes*	*pale pink flower*

ESERCIZIO
4·3

Identify each adjective as four-form, three-form, two-form, or one-form.

1. rosso _____

2. rosa _____

3. verde _____

4. blu _____

5. importante _____

6. pari _____

7. pessimista _____

8. viola _____

9. difficile _____

10. arancione _____

ESERCIZIO
4·4

Match the noun in the first column with the adjective from the second column that agrees in gender and number.

NOUN	ADJECTIVE
1. _____ il libro	a. francesi
2. _____ la casa	b. deliziosi
3. _____ l'automobile	c. ricco
4. _____ le amiche	d. interessante
5. _____ i mesi	e. tropicale
6. _____ gli studenti	f. spaziosa
7. _____ gli spaghetti	g. nuovo

8. _____ lo zio   h. italiane

9. _____ l'anno   i. veloce

10. _____ l'isola   j. invernali

Indefinite adjectives and pronouns

The following four-form adjectives are used to describe an indefinite quantity, and as we saw earlier, their endings change to agree with the noun.

poco	molto	troppo	tutto	altro
little	*much*	*too much*	*all*	*other*

Ho **molta** fame.   Ci sono **troppe** macchine.   Ci vediamo un'**altra** volta!
I'm very hungry.   *There are too many cars.*   *We'll see each other another time!*

Tutto means *all, whole* and is always followed by the definite article.

Tutti i giorni.   **Tutta** l'estate.   **Tutto** il tempo.
Every day.   *The whole summer.*   *The whole time.*

These adjectives are often used as pronouns, in which case the number and gender of the noun being replaced is used.

Avete mangiato **tutta** la torta?
Sì, l'abbiamo mangiata **tutta**!

Nessuno means *none* or *no one* and is always singular.

Non c'è ness**uno**?

Adjectives describing more than one noun

In general, when one adjective is being used to describe more than one noun of the same gender, the plural form of the common gender is used.

Anna e Mara sono italian**e**.
Roberto e Marco sono stanch**i**.

When two or more nouns do not share the same gender, the modifying adjective will be in the masculine plural form.

Roberto e Anna sono italian**i**.

The position of adjectives

Adjectives are generally placed *after* the noun in Italian, in a more emphatic position that makes the noun distinct from other nouns. This type of emphasis in English is achieved by stressing the adjective with the voice.

Il musicista **giovane** mi ha invitato al suo concerto.
*The **young** musician invited me to his concert.* (as opposed to the older one)

Quell'attrice porta gli occhiali da sole **molto grandi**.
*That actress is wearing **very large** sunglasses.*

Lo studente **italiano** parla bene l'inglese.
*The **Italian** student speaks English well.*

The same adjective before the noun is less important within the phrase and acquires a less restrictive and more descriptive function. Possessive, interrogative, demonstrative, and indefinite adjectives generally precede the noun.

il **mio** amico   **Quanti** corsi segui?   **queste** ragazze   un'**altra** volta

Pre-noun placement occurs frequently in idiomatic or everyday expressions and is often redundant.

il piccolo bambino	il ricco banchiere	la brava cantante
the small child	*the rich banker*	*the good singer*

un buon lavoro	un brutto affare	una buon'idea
a good job	*a terrible ordeal*	*a good idea*

Some adjectives actually change meaning depending on their positions.

un uomo grande	un grand'uomo
a big man	*a great man*

un prodotto caro	un caro amico
an expensive product	*a dear friend*

Nota bene

Although adjectives generally follow the noun, when they are modified by the adverb **molto**, they *always* follow the noun they modify.

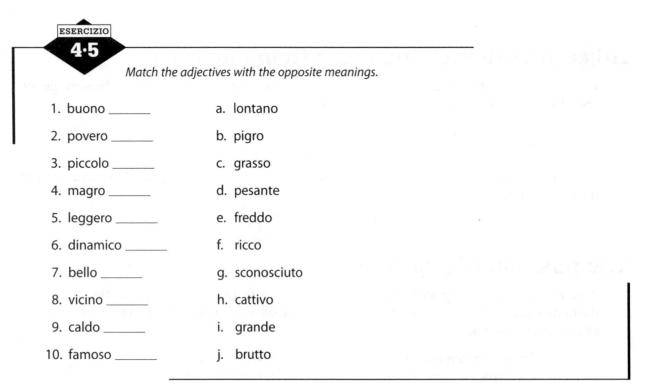

ESERCIZIO
4·5

Match the adjectives with the opposite meanings.

1. buono _____   a. lontano

2. povero _____   b. pigro

3. piccolo _____   c. grasso

4. magro _____   d. pesante

5. leggero _____   e. freddo

6. dinamico _____   f. ricco

7. bello _____   g. sconosciuto

8. vicino _____   h. cattivo

9. caldo _____   i. grande

10. famoso _____   j. brutto

Possessive adjectives

Possessive adjectives are used to denote possession and precede the noun they modify. Since the agreement is with the noun, the gender of the owner is not indicated by the adjective. Notice how **loro** is invariable and how all the possessives are regular except for the ones highlighted.

il mio	la mia	i **miei**	le mie
il tuo	la tua	i **tuoi**	le tue
il suo	la sua	i **suoi**	le tue
il nostro	la nostra	i nostri	le nostre
il vostro	la vostra	i vostri	le vostre
il loro	la loro	i loro	le loro

Il cane di Maria. → Il su**o cane.**   La giacca di Luigi. → La **sua** giacca.

If the article is preceded by **a**, **di**, **su**, or **in**, they combine into one word.

Il libro **di** + **la** mia professoressa. → Il libro **della** mia professoressa.

With singular and unmodified close relatives, the definite article is dropped, with the exception of the adjective **loro**.

mia sorella → **la** mia sorella minore → **le** mie sorelle → **la loro** sorella

Nota bene

The possessive adjectives are dropped with common possessions, such as **casa** (*home*), **la macchina** (*car*), **la bicicletta** (*bicycle*), **gli amici** (*friends*), and parts of the body, especially when used with reflexive verbs.

Tuo fratello si è messo **i guanti?**	*Did your brother put on (his) gloves?*
Quando ho aperto **gli occhi** . . .	*When I opened (my) eyes . . .*
Ti sei fatto male **al braccio?**	*Did you hurt (your) arm?*

I miei, **i tuoi**, and **i suoi**, when used without a noun, refer to one's parents.

Quando arrivano i tuoi?	*When are your (parents) getting back?*
I miei si sono conosciuti a Roma.	*My parents met in Rome.*

Comparative and superlative uses of the adjective

When making a comparison of inequality between two nouns, **più** or **meno** are placed before the adjective, which is generally followed by the preposition **di**. The subject generally appears at the beginning of the sentence, and the noun or pronoun it is being compared to follows the preposition **di**, with or without the article as the case may be.

Gaia è **più alta di** Susanna.	*Gaia is taller than Susanna.*
Venezia è **meno caotica delle** altre città che ho visitato.	*Venice is less chaotic than the other cities I visited.*
Carlo studia **più dei** suoi amici Giovanni e Marco.	*Carlo studies more than his friends Giovanni and Marco.*

Notice that in these sentences the comparison is followed by **di** + a noun, and two nouns are being compared in terms of the same quality or action.

In sentences where the comparison is being made between two adjectives, two pronouns, two adverbs, or two prepositional phrases (or any two terms that are the same parts of speech) in reference to one subject, **che** is used rather than **di**.

Marta è **più alta** *che* magra.	*but*	Marta è **più alta** *di* Gaia.
Ho cantato meno **in America** *che* in Italia.	*but*	Ho cantato **meno forte** *di* lei.
Mi piace più **leggere** *che* **giocare** a calcio.	*but*	Leggo **più** *di* Francesco.

Nota bene

When you're not sure whether to use **di** or **che**, remember that **di** will be preceded by an adjective and followed by a noun or pronoun, while **che** will link two words or phrases of the same part of speech.

ESERCIZIO
4·6

*Complete each sentence with **che** or **di** + article when needed.*

1. Anna è meno alta _____ Maria.

2. È più difficile guidare _____ prendere il treno.

3. Secondo me, il mare è più rilassante _____ stimolante.

4. In agosto la montagna è più tranquilla _____ spiaggia.

5. L'Italia ha più alberghi al nord _____ al sud.

6. Gli spaghetti ingrassano più _____ verdure.

7. Gli americani hanno meno ferie (*vacation*) _____ italiani.

8. Roma è più antica _____ New York.

9. Mi piace più cucinare _____ lavare i piatti.

10. Una Ferrari costa molto più _____ una Fiat.

Nota bene

If the second part of the comparison is a subordinate clause (it has another subject and conjugated verb), then **di quanto** + the subjunctive must be used. This type of sentence is rather complex and may be useful to more advanced speakers.

La campagna marchigiana è più bella **di quanto** immaginassi.
The Marche countryside is more beautiful than I imagined.

Equal comparisons

To make a comparison between two nouns that are equal, use:

> (**tanto**) + adjective + **quanto**

or

> (**così**) + adjective + **come**

The first adverb has been put in parentheses because it is optional. The adjective must agree with the subject and not with the noun it is being compared to, and the adverb, as always, is invariable.

> Isabella è **tanto** alta **quanto** Roberto. → Isabella è alta **quanto** Roberto.
> Isabella è **così** alta **come** Roberto. → Isabella è alta **come** Roberto.

ESERCIZIO
4·7

*Make comparisons of equality (=) or inequality (**più** +, **meno** −) using the appropriate form of the verb **essere** and the adjectives provided.*

1. Mario / + simpatico / Giacomo

   _____

2. le montagne / + alto / le colline

   _____

3. Giovanna / = studioso / sua sorella

   _____

4. Quell'attore / + bello / intelligente

   _____

5. autobus / = veloce / tram

   _____

6. spagnolo / + facile / francese

   _____

7. cani / + affettuosi / pescirossi (*goldfish*)

   _____

8. Cina / − grande / Russia

   _____

9. leggere la *Divina commedia* / + difficile / leggere *il Decameron*

   _____

10. Kobe Bryant / + famoso / Vasco Rossi

   _____

Absolute superlatives

Absolute superlatives are adjectives that are used to describe the quality of a noun without comparing it to any other noun. In English this is done by placing words such as *very* or *extremely* before the adjective. In Italian, words such as **molto**, **assai**, and **estremamente** have similar meaning and function.

Superlatives with -issimo/a/i/e

There is another form that is even more common in everyday speech, which is formed by adding the suffix -**issimo/a/i/e** to the adjective after dropping the final letter.

bello → bellissimo   elegante → elegantissimo*   largo → lar**gh**issimo**
simpatico → simpati**c**issimo**

---

*Notice that two-form adjectives, those ending with -**e** in the masculine and feminine singular, become four-form when the -**issimo** suffix is used.

The **c or **g** sound preceding the -**issimo** suffix acquires the same sound as the masculine plural form of the adjective, regardless of gender or number.

largo → lar**ghi** → lar**ghi**ssimo/a/i/e
simpatico → simpati**ci** → simpati**ci**ssimo/a/i/e

Irregular superlatives

In everyday speech the following adjectives are used to describe physical or material qualities of people or animals. In writing and in more figurative descriptions, the following irregular forms are also possible.

BASE ADJECTIVE	COMPARATIVE	SUPERLATIVE
alto	superiore	sommo
basso	inferiore	infimo
buono	migliore	ottimo
cattivo	peggiore	pessimo
grande	maggiore	massimo
piccolo	minore	minimo

ESERCIZIO
4·8

Reword the sentences using the irregular form of the adjective with a similar meaning.

1. I cornetti in quel bar sono **buoni**.

_____

2. Roberto è il fratello **più piccolo**.

_____

3. Salieri fu un compositore **poco importante**.

_____

4. Maradona è stato il calciatore **più bravo**.

_____

5. Abitano al piano di **sopra**.

_____

6. Quel film è di **cattivo** gusto.

_____

7. Quell'avvocato ha una **brutta** reputazione.

_____

8. Dante Alighieri è considerato il **più grande** poeta italiano.

_____

9. Gli spaghetti alla carbonara sono **buonissimi**!

_____

10. L'Orvieto Classico è **più buono** del vino della casa.

_____

ESERCIZIO
4·9

Reword the sentences using an adjective of the opposite meaning.

1. La casa è **piccola**.

_____

2. Questo pacco è **leggero**.

_____

3. Giovanni è un ragazzo **pigro**.

_____

4. Roberto è più **grasso** di Antonio.

_____

5. Questa strada è **stretta**.

_____

6. L'esame di chimica è **difficilissimo**!

_____

7. Nel negozio ho visto delle sedie **antiche**.

_____

8. La mia bici è **nuovissima**.

_____

9. Le mie amiche sono **tranquille**.

_____

10. Il **vecchio** professore è bravissimo.

_____

Adverbs

There are numerous types of adverbs that describe how, when, where, how much, or how often something is done and are often used in questions. They are much easier to use than adjectives because they are not marked for gender or number, and, therefore, have only one form. Adverbs can modify:

- A verb

    Francesco guida **velocemente**.   *Francesco drives **fast**.*

- An adjective

    Alida è un'attrice **estremamente**   *Alida is an **extremely** gifted*
    brava.   *actress.*

- An adverb or adverbial phrase

    Canta **molto** bene.   *He sings **very** nicely.*
    Sfortunatamente devo partire.   ***Unfortunately** I have to leave.*

Adverbs can be one word (**oggi, qui, quando, come**, etc.), compound words (that is, single words that are combined—**perché, soprattutto**, etc.), words that are derived from adjectives (**veramente, generalmente, probabilmente**), and adverbial phrases (**in fretta, di corsa**, etc.). Adverbs often describe how something is done.

As you can see from the earlier examples, many adverbs end in **-mente**, which generally corresponds to the English suffix *-ly*. The stem of these adverbs is always an adjective, which can be turned into an adverb by following these simple rules:

- Four-form adjectives: change the adjective to the feminine form and add the suffix -**mente**.

    vero → vera + mente →   allegro → allegra + mente →
       veramente   **allegramente**

- Two-form adjectives not ending in -**le** or -**re**: simply add -**mente**.

    breve + mente →   semplice + mente →
       brevemente   **semplicemente**

- Adjectives ending in -**le** and -**re**: simply drop the final -**e** and add -**mente**.

    naturale → **naturalmente**   speciale → **specialmente**
    probabile → **probabilmente**

There are a few exceptions, the most common being:

leggero → **leggermente**   violento → **violentemente**

Some important adverbs are not derived from an adjective.

bene   male   insieme   così   volentieri

Some adverbs and adjectives share the same form. Look at these two examples:

La musica **forte** non mi piace. (adj.)
Parla **piano**! (adv.)

Different types of adverbs

Some adverbs answer questions starting with *where*? *when*? and *how much*? Here is a list of common adverbs that answer questions starting with:

+ **Dove** (*Where*)?

Dove siete?	*Where are you?*	Siamo qui!	*We're over here!*
qui, qua	*here*	lì, là	*there*
giù	*down*	su	*up there*
vicino	*near*	lontano	*far*
dentro	*inside*	fuori	*outside*
davanti	*in front of*	dietro	*behind*
sopra	*above*	sotto	*beneath*

+ **Quando** (*When*)?

Quando andiamo?	*When are we going?*	Domani sera.	*Tomorrow night.*
oggi	*today*	domani	*tomorrow*
ieri	*yesterday*	dopodomani	*the day after tomorrow*
ora, adesso	*now*	fra poco	*in a little while*
prima	*before*	dopo	*later*
sempre	*always*	mai	*never*
presto	*soon*	tardi	*late*

+ **Quanto** (*How much*)?

Quanto costa?	*How much does it cost?*	Costa molto.	*It costs a lot.*
molto, tanto	*a lot*	un po', un poco, poco	*a little*
più	*more*	meno	*less*
abbastanza, piuttosto	*rather, enough*	troppo	*too much*
quasi	*almost*		

Nota bene

The words underlined above can also function as adjectives. Remember, when used as adjectives they must agree with the noun they are describing. With **molto**, remember that if **molto** means *very* (adv.) it "doesn't vary."

Ho **molti** amici italiani. (adj.)   Sono **molto** stanca. (adv.)
I have a many Italian friends.   *I am very tired.*

Scrivo **poche** lettere. (adj.)   Pollini lo suona **un poco** più velocemente. (adv.)
I write few letters.   *Pollini plays it a little faster.*

Some adverbs replace the simple affirmative **sì**.

Vuoi andare a vedere un film?	**Certo!**
Do you want to go see a movie?	*Sure!*

Some adverbs indicate agreement.

esattamente	precisamente	appunto	davvero
exactly	*precisely*	*right*	*really*

The adverbs **mica**, **niente**, and **mai** make negative phrases more emphatic.

non è vero	*it's not true*	non è **mica** vero	*it's not true **at all***
non c'entra	*it doesn't have to do with*	non c'entra **niente**	*it doesn't have **anything** to do with it*
non ho detto questo	*I didn't say this*	non ho **mai** detto questo	*I **never** said this*

Adding these adverbs to your conversation is not difficult and will make it sound more native. As you see from the examples, they almost always follow the verb in the present tense, and they follow the auxiliary in the compound tenses.

Proverbi che usano avverbi

Chi va **piano** va sano e **lontano**.
He who goes slowly goes healthy and far.

Lontano dagli occhi, **lontano** dal cuore.
Far from the eyes, far from the heart.

ESERCIZIO
5·1

Change the following adjectives into adverbs.

1. relativo _____

2. breve _____

3. esatto _____

4. vero _____

5. semplice _____

6. possibile _____

7. raro _____

8. franco _____

9. diretto _____

10. probabile _____

Match each question with its answer. Note any adverbs you find in the questions or answers.

1. Quando vanno in vacanza? _____   a. Perché voglio andare a Roma.

2. Abiti ancora a Milano? _____   b. Fortunatamente sì.

3. Perché studi l'italiano? _____   c. Ci siamo andati spessissimo.

4. Come guida tuo fratello? _____   d. Generalmente in agosto.

5. Quanto vuole per questa sedia? _____   e. Non ci abito più da un anno.

6. Ha già trovato un lavoro? _____   f. La vendo a poco . . . 40 euro.

7. Come si chiama quella ragazza? _____   g. Ci vado raramente.

8. Vai spesso a teatro? _____   h. Certamente!

9. Siete mai andati in montagna? _____   i. Corre troppo.

10. Mi presti cento euro? _____   j. Veramente non l'ho mai vista.

The following sentences each answer a question introduced by the adverbs **quando**, **perché**, **quanto**, **dove**, or **come**. Give the most logical question to each answer, using no more than four words.

1. L'inverno comincia in dicembre.

_____

2. Claudia è alta e bionda.

_____

3. Il pane costava pochissimo.

_____

4. Non so perché si arrabbia.

_____

5. Tornerà la settimana prossima.

_____

6. Le lezioni vanno benissimo, grazie.

_____

7. Abitava a Venezia.

_____

8. Mette la macchina in un garage vicino a casa sua.

_____

ESERCIZIO
5·4

Change the boldfaced phrases in the following sentences into one of the adverbs from the list with the same meaning. There are two extra words.

velocemente   veramente   sempre   pochissimo   seriamente

spesso   divinamente   piano   raramente   sfortunatamente

1. Vado al cinema **una volta l'anno**.

_____

2. Con la mia Ferrari guido **a 100 chilometri all'ora**.

_____

3. Mangia la pasta **a pranzo e a cena**.

_____

4. Amedeo **non** parla **forte**.

_____

5. Giacomo studia **il meno possibile** ma prende sempre 100!

_____

6. Vado in palestra **tre o quattro volte a settimana**.

_____

7. Paola studiava **con molta serietà**.

_____

8. Suona il violino **in modo divino**.

_____

Complete the answers with the opposite adverb.

1. Guidi troppo **velocemente**!

   Ma no, guido _____!

2. Parli **sempre** al telefono!

   Ma no, non parlo _____!

3. Sei così **fortunata**!

   Ma no, sono _____!

4. Ti sta **malissimo** l'arancione!

   Ma no, mi sta _____!

5. Mangiamo **fuori**?

   Ma no, mangiamo _____!

6. Studi **poco**!

   Ma no, studio _____!

7. Ceniamo **prima** del concerto?

   Ma no, ceniamo _____!

8. Arrivi sempre **tardi**!

   Ma no, arrivo sempre _____!

Introduction to verb tenses

Every verb has a stem (which stays the same in regular verbs) and an ending (which changes according to the subject). Italian can omit the subject pronoun because the ending of the conjugated verb indicates the subject. This makes the subject pronoun unnecessary. In the conjugations in this chapter, the subject pronoun is in parentheses to remind you of this.

The three conjugations: -are, -ere, -ire

Verbs of the first conjugation are the most frequent and end in -**are**. It is also the conjugation that accommodates the many new verbs imported from the fields of finance, popular culture, and technology. These include:

scannerizzare	*to scan*
monitorare	*to monitor*
chattare	*to chat* (*online*)
cliccare	*to click*

Verbs of the second conjugation end in -**ere**, are the least frequent, and, contrary to the other conjugations, are stressed on either the stem (third-to-last syllable) or the infinitive ending (second-to-last syllable).

prendere	*to take*	scegliere	*to choose*	leggere	*to read*
vedere	*to see*	sapere	*to know*	dovere	*must, to have to*

Verbs of the third conjugation end in -**ire** and include the subgroup that use -**isc** between the stem and the suffix.

essere and avere

The two most important verbs in Italian are **essere** (*to be*) and **avere** (*to have*). Besides their meanings (*to be* and *to have*), they are also used as auxiliaries. This means that they combine with other verbs to create compound tenses.

essere		avere	
sono	siamo	ho	abbiamo
sei	siete	hai	avete
è	sono	ha	hanno

essere

Essere means *to be*, *to exist*, or *to be located*.

È italiano, di Roma.   *He **is** Italian, from Rome.*
Sono Susanna.   *I **am** Susanna.*

Esserci, a form of the verb **essere** that combines **ci** + **essere**, is used to express the presence of things or people in a place, and often precedes the subject. **Ci** is elided with the forms of **essere** that start with a vowel.

C'è un buon film stasera?   ***Is there** a good film tonight?*
Ci sono molti musicisti alla festa.   ***There are** many musicians at the party.*
C'è Roberto?   ***Is** Roberto **there**?*

We may also use this form when asking whether something is available, for example:

Ci sono gli spaghetti al pomodoro?   *Is there (Do you have) spaghetti with tomato sauce?*

ESERCIZIO
6·1

*Complete each sentence with the conjugated form of either **essere** or **ci** + **essere**.*

1. Non _____ montagne a Chicago.

2. _____ il vino bianco fresco?

3. Il vino bianco _____ fresco?

4. _____ Maria? No, non _____. È a casa dei suoi genitori.

5. _____ un buon profumo di caffè!

6. Dove _____ i ragazzi? Marco _____ al cinema con i suoi amici,

   e Valentina _____ a casa a studiare.

7. _____ un piccolo problema.

8. _____ ancora i cavalli selvatici in Abruzzo?

---

avere

Avere means *to have*, *to possess*, or *to obtain* and expresses certain states of being or feeling.

avere fame   *to be hungry*
avere sete   *to be thirsty*
avere paura (di)   *to be afraid (of)*

For more on the use of **essere** and **avere** as auxiliary verbs, see Chapter 7.

Idiomatic uses of avere

Many common expressions that use *to be* in English use **avere** in Italian. Notice that in English, all of the following expressions, except for the first one, use *to be* + adjective. In Italian, they use *to have* + noun and they express what one experiences, rather than how one feels: *to be hungry* is *to have hunger*, etc.

avere (*to have*)		to be	
avere _____ anni		*to be _____ years old*	
avere caldo		*to be hot*	
avere fame		*to be hungry*	
avere freddo		*to be cold*	
avere fretta		*to be in a hurry*	
avere paura		*to be afraid*	
avere ragione		*to be right*	
avere sete		*to be thirsty*	
avere sonno		*to be sleepy*	
avere torto		*to be wrong*	

Nota bene

You will learn these expressions more effectively by using them in simple sentences rather than memorizing the infinitive form out of context.

Other useful idioms that use **avere** are:

avere a che fare	*to have to do with*
avere da fare	*to be busy*
avere da ridire	*to object to something* (often used in the negative)

ESERCIZIO
6·2

Answer the following questions by using an expression with the opposite meaning. If you do not know the word with the opposite meaning, use the same verb in the negative.

ESEMPIO   Hai freddo?

No, ho caldo. or *No, non ho freddo.*

1. Il professore ha ragione? _____

2. Gli studenti hanno fretta? _____

3. Avete fame? _____

4. Hai paura dei ragni (*spiders*)? _____

5. Hai sete la mattina presto? _____

6. Il tennista ha freddo quando gioca? _____

7. Quando nuoti (*swim*) nel lago, hai caldo? _____

8. Gli studenti hanno troppo da fare? _____

Translate the following phrases into Italian, omitting pronouns as necessary.

1. *I'm hungry!*

_____

2. *You're right.*

_____

3. *She's cold.*

_____

4. *We're in a hurry.*

_____

5. *Are you 21?*

_____

6. *We're not thirsty.*

_____

7. *Are you (plural) hot?*

_____

8. *She's sleepy.*

_____

9. *I'm scared!*

_____

10. *They're wrong.*

_____

*Complete each sentence with the correct idiomatic expression of **avere**.*

1. Quando (noi) _____ , beviamo l'acqua minerale.

2. Quando (io) _____ , dormo!

3. Quando (loro) _____ , prendono un tassì.

4. Quando (tu) _____ , chiedi scusa.

5. Quando (lei) _____ al cinema, chiude gli occhi.

6. Quando (io) _____, mangio pane e salame.

7. Quando (voi) _____, accendete l'aria condizionata.

8. Quando (noi) _____, accendiamo il riscaldamento (*heat*).

Verb tenses

Every simple tense (single verb) corresponds to a compound tense (auxiliary + participle), except for the imperative (which is always in the present). When you have learned all the verb forms, make sure you understand what they mean and how they are used. Many tenses used in Italian (such as the imperfect, past perfect, future perfect, and subjunctive) are not commonly used in spoken English. This creates a barrier for English speakers, as they learn tenses that they have never used in English or have never had to identify grammatically. It is useful to get to know the names and uses of the simple and compound tenses as you learn the forms in the next chapter.

SIMPLE TENSES	COMPOUND TENSES
I. INDICATIVE	
present	present perfect
imperfect	past perfect
remote past	past pluperfect
future	future perfect
imperative	
II. SUBJUNCTIVE	
present	past
imperfect	pluperfect
III. CONDITIONAL	
present	past conditional
IV. INFINITIVE	
present	past infinitive
V. GERUND	
present	past

After you have become familiar with how the verbs are used, revisit this list and drill the problematic ones until they become easy and automatic. For example, starting with **essere** in the first person, the drill will be:

I. sono, sono stato/a/i/e
   ero, ero stato/a/i/e
   fui, fui stato/a/i/e
   sarò, sarò stato/a/e/i
   (No imperative in the first person.)

II. sia, sia stato
    fossi, fossi stato/a/i/e

III. sarei, sarei stato/a/i/e

IV. essere, essere stato/a/i/e

V. stando, essendo stato/a/i/e

If drilling all the tenses proves too difficult at first, a simpler option is to focus on one tense at a time and to drill different verbs in the tense that needs practice. For example, the irregular verbs **bere**, **dire**, **essere**, and **fare** in the imperfect can be harder to learn, and you can drill them (written or spoken) in all six persons:

> bevevo, bevevi ...
> ero, eri ...
> dicevo, dicevi ...
> facevo, facevi ...

After practicing this way you can return to the more communicative exercises for each tense and repeat them. You will see an improvement in accuracy and speed in your writing and speaking skills.

Present and present perfect tenses

The three conjugations are recognizable from the last three letters of the verb. Regular verbs follow the patterns presented in this chapter and do not change their stems or roots. Irregular verbs change their stems and follow patterns that are generally determined by their Latin origins. The two most important irregular verbs are **avere** and **essere** (see Chapter 6).

Regular -are verbs

Verbs of the first conjugation end in -**are** and are the most common verb type in Italian. In regular -**are** verbs, the person, or subject, is indicated by the suffix, or ending, which is added to the stem. The present tense (**il presente**) form is as follows:

parlare (*to speak*)			
(io)	**parl**-o	(noi)	parl-**iamo**
(tu)	**parl**-i	(voi)	parl-**ate**
(lei/lui)	**parl**-a	(loro)	**parl**-ano

The syllables in bold show where the stress falls. This pattern is the same in all three conjugations. The stem is stressed in all persons except for the **noi** and **voi** forms. It may be easier to remember that all the forms are stressed on the penultimate, or second-to-last, syllable, except for the third-person plural, which is stressed on the third-to-last syllable.

> ### Nota bene
> When practicing the verbs, remember that the *third*-person plural is stressed on the *third*-to-last syllable.

Notes on -are verbs

Verbs ending in -**care** and -**gare** always retain their hard **c** and **g** sounds, so an -**h** is added when the suffix starts with the softening vowels -**i** or -**e**.

pago	paghiamo
paghi	pagate
paga	pagano

Verbs that end in **-ciare**, **-giare**, or **-sciare** drop the initial **-i** of the stem when the ending begins with an **-e** or **-i**.

comincio	cominciamo
cominci	cominciate
comincia	cominciano

In the participle form, the soft sound is kept and, therefore, the **-i** remains.

cominciato   festeggiato   mangiato   lasciato

In verbs that have an accented **-i**, such as **invio** or **scio** (rhymes with **mio**), the extra **-i** is kept when a suffix beginning with an **-i** is added.

invii   scii

One **-i** is dropped when it falls on an unaccented syllable.

inviamo   sciamo

The verbs ending in **-gliare** drop the **-i** of the stem before endings that start with **-i**, but keep it if the ending begins with **-a**, **-e**, or **-u**.

sbagli   consigli   sbadigli   *but*   sbaglierò   consiglierei   sbadiglieranno

Regular -ere verbs

Most irregular verbs belong to this (second) conjugation. The stress pattern in **-ere** verbs can be of two types. In the infinitive form, some verbs have the stress on the penultimate syllable (**vedere, temere**) similar to the **-are** verbs, but most have the stress on the stem (**vendere, prendere, spendere**), or the third-to-last syllable.

prendere (*to take*)			
(io)	**prend**-o	(noi)	prend-**iamo**
(tu)	**prend**-i	(voi)	prend-ete
(lei, lui)	**prend**-e	(loro)	**prend**-ono

Pronunciation tips

Contrary to the **-are** verbs, verbs ending in **-cere**, **-gere**, or **-scere** harden the soft **-c**, **-g**, and **-sc** of the infinitive when followed by a suffix beginning with a letter other than **-e** or **-i**.

leggere (*to read*)			
(io)	**legg**-o	(noi)	legg-**iamo**
(tu)	**legg**-i	(voi)	legg-ete
(lei/lui)	**legg**-e	(loro)	**legg**-ono

Therefore, the first-person singular and the third-person plural are pronounced with the hard **c** or **g**, while the remaining forms retain the soft sound of the infinitive. In regular verbs, such as **conoscere** and **piacere**, an **-i** is added to the participle to keep the soft sound.

conoscere → conosciuto   piacere → piaciuto

Regular -ire verbs

Verbs of the third conjugation share the same endings as -**ere** verbs, except for the **voi** form.

dormire (*to sleep*)			
(io)	**dorm**-o	(noi)	dorm-**iamo**
(tu)	**dorm**-i	(voi)	dorm-ite
(lei/lui)	**dorm**-e	(loro)	**dorm**-ono

-isc verbs

There is a group of the -**ire** verbs that adds -**isc** between the stem and the ending in first-, second-, and third-person singular and third-person plural. Most verbs of this type (**capire, finire, ferire, preferire, pulire**) tend to have one consonant and vowel just before the -**ire** ending.

finire (*to finish*)			
(io)	fin-**isc**-o (sk)	(noi)	fin-**ia**mo
(tu)	fin-**isc**-i (sh)	(voi)	fin-ite
(lei/lui)	fin-**isc**-e (sh)	(loro)	fin-**isc**-ono (sk)

Nota bene

Remember that in -**isc** verbs, the **c** sound is pronounced as a *k* in the first-person singular and third-person plural, and as *sh* in all the other forms.

The -**isc** is added only in the present tense, but not in the participial or the gerund.

capito   finito   ferito   preferendo

Proverbi nel tempo presente (*Proverbs that feature the present tense*)

Il tempo porta consiglio.	*Time brings advice.*
Troppi cuochi guastano la minestra.	*Too many cooks spoil the soup.*
Il cane che abbaia non morde.	*The dog that barks doesn't bite.*

ESERCIZIO
7·1

Indicate the correct forms of the missing verbs.

AMARE (*TO LOVE*)	VEDERE (*TO SEE*)	OFFRIRE (*TO OFFER*)	CAPIRE (*TO UNDERSTAND*)
amo	_____	_____	capisco
_____	vedi	_____	_____
_____	_____	offre	_____
_____	_____	_____	capiamo
_____	vedete	_____	_____
amano	_____	_____	_____

Present tense irregular verbs

The verbs listed below include some frequently used irregular verbs from each conjugation. A complete list can be found on the many Italian language websites by searching *irregular Italian verbs*.

andare (*to go*)	fare (*to do*)	avere (*to have*)	essere (*to be*)	rimanere (*to remain*)	tenere (*to keep*)
vado	faccio	ho	sono	**rimango**	tengo
vai	fai	hai	sei	rimani	tieni
va	fa	ha	è	rimane	tiene
andiamo	facciamo	abbiamo	siamo	rimaniamo	teniamo
andate	fate	avete	siete	rimanete	tenete
vanno	fanno	hanno	sono	**rimangono**	tengono

dire (*to say*)	uscire (*to go out*)	venire (*to come*)
dico	**esco**	**vengo**
dici	esci	**vieni**
dice	esce	**viene**
diciamo	usciamo	veniamo
dite	**uscite**	**venite**
dicono	**escono**	**vengono**

Some students learn irregular verb forms through memorization, while others prefer to learn them in context. I recommend a combination of both. As you read and study these verbs, try to make a mental note and analyze the patterns you see, grouping together verbs with similar patterns. For example, if you look at the first and last person of these verbs, what do you notice? Here are three patterns that will help you use these verb forms correctly:

1. The first-person singular and the third-person plural are almost always identical except for the last syllable (-**no**) of the third-person plural.

2. The **voi** form always uses the regular infinitive stem, except for **essere**.

3. The verbs **venire** and **tenere** follow the same pattern with the letter **g** added in the first-person singular and the third-person plural, and the letter **i** added in the second- and third-person singular.

Complete the chart with the missing forms of the irregular verbs.

ANDARE		FARE		AVERE	
vado	_____	faccio	_____	_____	abbiamo
_____	_____	_____	fate	_____	_____
_____	vanno	_____	_____	ha	hanno

ESSERE		TENERE		BERE	
_____	_____	tengo	_____	_____	_____
_____	siete	_____	_____	bevi	_____
è	_____	_____	_____	_____	bevono

DIRE		USCIRE		VENIRE	
_____	_____	esco	_____	vengo	_____
dici	dite	_____	uscite	_____	_____
		_____		_____	vengono

Uses of the present tense (il presente)

The use of the present tense in Italian and English is for the most part very similar. It is important to remember, however, that in English the present continuous (*I am working*) and the simple present (*I work, I do work*) correspond to the just one tense in Italian. This means that the question **"Che cosa fai?"** in Italian can be translated as either "What are you doing?" or "What do you do?" Depending on the context, the answers to the question may vary. Below is a list of situations in which the present tense is commonly used.

♦ An event happening in the present or the near future

> Torno a Roma.
> *I am returning to Rome.*

♦ A repeated or ongoing action

> Di solito studio in biblioteca.
> *I usually study in the library.*

♦ A current state of being and condition

> Sono americana e vivo a Venezia.
> *I am American and I live in Venice.*

The following words and phrases often accompany or trigger the use of verbs in the present tense:

di solito	*usually*
domani	*tomorrow*

fra poco	*soon*
oggi	*today*
ora, adesso	*now*
stasera	*this evening, tonight*

ESERCIZIO 7·3

Compose sentences using the correct form of the irregular verbs in parentheses.

1. Anna (andare) . . .

_____

2. Gli italiani (essere) . . .

_____

3. Io (bere) . . .

_____

4. Rob e Cecilia (venire) . . .

_____

5. Tu e Marco (rimanere) . . .

_____

6. Io e Susanna (dire) . . .

_____

7. Lei, Signora Rossellini, (uscire) . . .

_____

8. Tu, Maria, (fare) . . .

_____

Proverbi con verbi irregolari

L'unione **fa** la forza.	*Unity makes strength.*
L'occasione **fa** l'uomo ladro.	*Opportunity makes the man a thief.*
Una rondine non **fa** primavera.	*One swallow doesn't make spring.*
Le bugie **hanno** le gambe corte.	*Lies have short legs. (They don't run very far.)*
Al buio tutti i gatti sono bigi.	*In the dark all cats are grey.*

The present perfect tense (il passato prossimo)

The present perfect (**il passato prossimo**) is used to describe actions completed in the recent past. It is a compound tense made up of an auxiliary verb (**essere** or **avere**) and the past participle of the main verb. The **passato prossimo** corresponds to two tenses in English.

Ho studiato l'italiano can be translated as:

I studied Italian. (simple past)

or

I have studied Italian. (present perfect)

The auxiliary verb combine with the past participle of the main verb form to form compound tenses, such as the present perfect (**ho mangiato, sono andato/a**), the past conditional (**avrei mangiato, sarei andato**), the future perfect (**avrò mangiato, sarò andato**), and others.

Knowing which auxiliary the verb requires can be difficult at first, but through frequent use and repetition this will become automatic. When in doubt, however, it may help to remember that the great majority of verbs use **avere**.

Nota bene

You will be able to use the auxiliaries more fluently if you review the simple tenses before learning each new compound tense.

avere as an auxiliary verb

Most verbs are transitive verbs, can be used with an object, and take the auxiliary verb **avere**. It is used:

♦ With compound forms of **avere**

abbiamo avuto	avevo avuto	avresti avuto
we had	*I had had*	*you would have had*

♦ With all transitive verbs

Ho mangiato una mela.	Hai letto un libro.
I ate an apple.	*You read a book.*

♦ With a few intransitive verbs

Ho lavorato.	Hanno viaggiato.	Avresti dormito.
I worked.	*They traveled.*	*You would have slept.*

Nota bene

Although these verbs cannot be used with an object, and are therefore intransitive, they are unusual in that they use **avere** as the auxiliary. Here is a list of some other intransitive verbs that use **avere** in compound tenses:

ballare
pranzare
cenare
dormire
piangere
ridere
lavorare
camminare
passeggiare
nuotare
viaggiare

*Using the two model sentences, compose sentences using the **presente** and **passato prossimo** of the given verb. All the verbs are transitive and will use **avere** as their auxiliary.*

ESEMPIO   studiare

Oggi studio l'italiano.

Anche ieri ho studiato l'italiano.

1. parlare con il professore

_____

_____

2. telefonare alla zia

_____

_____

3. capire la lezione

_____

_____

4. vendere qualcosa su eBay

_____

_____

5. avere freddo

_____

_____

6. guardare la TV

_____

_____

7. ascoltare la radio

_____

_____

8. finire la lezione

_____

_____

9. ballare il tango

_____

_____

10. preferire il cappuccino

_____

_____

Modals and auxiliaries

In standard Italian, modal verbs take the auxiliary of the verb that follows the modal.

> Main verb takes **avere** → **Hai** dovuto **lavorare** fino a tardi?
> _Did you have to work until late?_

> Main verb takes **essere** → **Sei** dovuto **rimanere** fino a tardi?
> _Did you have to stay late?_

In everyday speech, however, this rule is often disregarded. This is another example of how _prescriptive grammar_, where rules are prescribed by grammarians, does not always match _descriptive grammar_, where rules are based on forms that speakers actually use.

> Descriptive grammar → **Hai** dovuto **rimanere** fino a tardi? _Did you have to stay late?_

Nota bene

The written language tends to be more conservative and does not always reflect the changes that occur in the spoken language. In academic or literary speech, prescriptive forms are preferred and should be used whenever there is any doubt.

More on modals

A modal verb followed by a reflexive verb takes **essere** as the auxiliary when the pronoun precedes the modal, as in the following example:

> **Si sono dovuti** salutare alla stazione.
> _They had to say good-bye at the station._

But it takes **avere** when the pronoun is attached to the infinitive:

> **Hanno dovuto salutarsi** alla stazione.
> _They had to say good-bye at the station._

Transitive verbs

If a verb can be used with an object, it generally uses the auxiliary **avere** in compound tenses. The verb **bere** (_to drink_) is an example of a transitive verb. The object in this case answers the question _What_ do you drink? The direct object **acqua** answers that question.

Bevo l'acqua.	_I drink the water._
Ho bevuto l'acqua.	_I drank the water._
Avevo bevuto l'acqua.	_I had drunk the water._
Avrei bevuto l'acqua.	_I would have drunk the water._
Avrò bevuto l'acqua.	_I will have drunk the water._

Intransitive verbs

If a verb *cannot* be used with an object, then it generally takes **essere** as the auxiliary in all compound tenses, with the last letter of the participle changing to agree in gender and number with the subject. The following sentences in the **passato prossimo** (*present perfect*) illustrate the agreement of the participle with the subject.

Sono andat**o**.   (masculine singular)
I went.

Sono andat**a**.   (feminine singular)
I went.

Siamo andat**i**.   (masculine plural)
We went.

Siamo andat**e**.   (feminine plural)
We went.

Vado a casa.
I am going home.

Sono andato/andata a casa.
I went home.

Ero andato/andata a casa.
I had gone home.

Saremmo andati/andate a casa.
We would have gone home.

Saranno andati/andate a casa.
They will have gone home.

Idioms with the present perfect

When asking how something went and there is no inherent subject in the sentence, the participle generally has a feminine ending. If there is a subject, then the regular agreement occurs.

Com'**è andata**?	*How did it go?*
Com'**è andato** il viaggio?	*How did **the trip** go?*

essere as an auxiliary verb

The auxiliary **essere** requires agreement of the participle in gender and number with the subject. It is used:

* With compound forms of **essere**

È stat**o** un malinteso.	Isabella sarà stat**a** qui un'ora fa.
It was a misunderstanding.	*Isabella must have been here an hour ago.*

* With reflexive and pronominal verbs (verbs that are preceded by a pronoun)

Mi sono svegliato.	Ci siamo ricordati.
I woke up.	*We remembered.*

- With most intransitive verbs

    Siamo partiti presto.
    We left early.

    È uscito poco fa.
    He went out a while ago.

- With the passive voice

    È stato costruito in tre anni.
    It was built in three years.

    I ragazzi **sono stati** invitati.
    The kids were invited.

ESERCIZIO

7·5

Create two sentences using the **presente** and the **passato prossimo** of the given verbs, following the model. All the following verbs take **essere**, so be careful to make the agreement.

ESEMPIO   Maria / andare

Oggi Maria va a scuola.

Anche ieri è andata a scuola.

1. Antonio (tornare) tardi

_____

_____

2. Amelia (svegliarsi) presto

_____

_____

3. Tu e Amedeo (partire) per Napoli

_____

_____

4. Paola e Francesca (andare) a scuola

_____

_____

5. Voi (uscire) alle 7.30

_____

_____

6. Io e i miei amici (andare) al cinema

_____

_____

7. I ragazzi (restare) a casa

_____

_____

8. Paola (passare) a casa mia

_____

_____

9. Guglielmo non (tornare) a New York

_____

_____

10. Regina (partire) con Sandro

_____

_____

*Change the following sentences from the **presente** to the **passato prossimo**, remembering the agreement for the intransitive verbs.*

1. Anna deve andare a New York.

_____

2. Puoi telefonare a Marco?

_____

3. Amelia vuole venire a casa.

_____

4. I ragazzi possono tornare.

_____

5. Devo lavorare fino a tardi.

_____

6. Vogliono andare al mare.

_____

7. Non posso venire a cena.

_____

8. Te e Anna dovete leggere questo libro.

_____

Verbs that can take either **essere** or **avere**

Some verbs can function as either transitive or intransitive verbs, and their auxiliary changes accordingly. These include: **cominciare, finire, cambiare, passare**. If the subject is a person and takes an object, the verb is transitive and takes **avere**. If the subject is a thing or cannot take an object, then it is intransitive and takes **essere**. Notice that in the left column, there are no objects, while on the right, the verbs are followed by a direct object.

INTRANSITIVE	TRANSITIVE
Il film **è cominciato** tardi. *The film started late.*	Susanna **ha cominciato** il libro ieri. *Susanna started the book yesterday.*
L'inverno **è passato**. *Winter has passed.*	Gaia **ha passato** l'estate in Grecia. *Gaia passed the summer in Greece.*
Lo stile di Armani non **è cambiato**. *Armani's style has not changed.*	Susanna **ha cambiato** l'abito. *Susanna changed her dress.*
L'acqua bolle! *The water is boiling!*	**Ho bollito** le uova per tre minuti. *I boiled the eggs for three minutes.*
Il tempo **è cambiato**. *The weather has changed.*	Marco **ha cambiato** lavoro. *He changed jobs.*
Il film **è finito** a mezzanotte. *The film ended at midnight.*	**Ho finito** il libro ieri sera. *I finished the book yesterday.*

Nota bene

Verbs related to the weather can take either **essere** or **avere**.

Ieri **ha** piovuto. *Yesterday it rained.*	Ieri **è** piovuto. *Yesterday it rained.*

ESERCIZIO

7·7

*Decide whether the following sentences are transitive or intransitive and change them to the **passato prossimo** using either **avere** or **essere**.*

1. L'opera finisce tardi.

   _____

2. Maria comincia il lavoro.

   _____

3. La situazione cambia.

   _____

4. Marco passa davanti a casa mia.

   _____

5. Lucia e Bob ritornano sabato.

   _____

6. Riporto il libro in biblioteca.

_____

7. Il tempo cambia in autunno.

_____

8. La musica finisce.

_____

9. Il presidente comincia il suo discorso.

_____

10. Passiamo l'estate in Italia.

_____

Irregular participles

Most -**are** verbs have regular participles, but some -**ere** and -**ire** verbs change the stem slightly in forming the participle. The best way to learn these irregular forms is to look closely at the patterns and to use them in writing and speaking. They have been divided according to their conjugation and pattern similarities. Try to identify in what way they are irregular and why they are grouped the way they are.

-are

fare → fatto
dare → dato
stare → stato

-ere (remember that most -ere verbs are stressed on the third-to-last syllable)

accendere → acceso
offendere → offeso
chiudere → chiuso
decidere → deciso
dividere → diviso
prendere → preso
scendere* → sceso
bere → bevuto
chiedere → chiesto
rimanere** → rimasto
rispondere → risposto
vedere → visto
essere** → stato
nascere** → nato
correre* → corso
perdere → perso

---

*Verbs that take **essere** or **avere**
Verbs that take **essere

leggere → letto
rompere → rotto
scrivere → scritto
mettere → messo
vivere* → vissuto
succedere** → successo
spegnere → spento
vincere → vinto

-ire

aprire → aperto
offrire → offerto
dire → detto
morire** → morto
venire** → venuto
tradurre → tradotto
produrre → prodotto

*Verbs that take **essere** or **avere**
Verbs that take **essere

ESERCIZIO

7·8

Create ten sentences about yourself using only irregular participles. If your experiences do not include some verbs, use them in a negative sentence. Be careful to use the correct auxiliary!

ESEMPIO   *Sono nata a Roma.*

Ho visto Parigi, Vienna e Budapest.

Ho letto un libro di Michela Murgia.

1. _____
2. _____
3. _____
4. _____
5. _____
6. _____
7. _____
8. _____
9. _____
10. _____

Imperfect and past perfect tenses

In this chapter we will look at the imperfect tense, which is used frequently in Italian but does not have a corresponding tense in English, and the past perfect, which does exist in English. In English, the imperfect is usually expressed with *would* + main verb and indicates a repeated or customary action.

> *After school I **would go** to the café to meet my friends.* (This action occurred frequently.)

Nota bene

In English, the imperfect is easily confused with the conditional. Notice the difference in meaning between the above sentence and the following one, even though the verb tense seems to be identical:

> *I **would go** to the café if I had the money.* (This action has not occurred, and is dependent on a condition. In Italian, the conditional tense would be used.)

The past perfect, or **trapassato prossimo**, is used to express an action in the past that took place before another action in the past, and therefore clarifies the order in which these actions occurred. This tense exists in English but is not often used in everyday speech.

The imperfect (l'imperfetto)

Learning the different forms of the imperfect (**l'imperfetto**) is not difficult, since it is a tense that has few irregular forms. Since English does not have a tense for recurring or continuous actions in the past, it can prove challenging to know how and when to use it. While other past-tense forms are used to describe completed events, the **imperfetto** tends to describe how things were or used to be. Let us look at some examples illustrating when this tense is used.

In the first example a recurring event is being described, and the use of the imperfect is accompanied by the phrase "in the summer." We do not know how many times this event occurred, but the **imperfetto** indicates it was not a single event but a recurring event in the summertime. If "in the summer" were omitted, the **imperfetto** alone would be enough to express that this was not one isolated event but one that recurred many times.

> D'estate **andavamo** al mare.　　*In the summer we would go to the beach.*

The **imperfetto** is also used to describe an ongoing event that was occurring when another single event occurred. In this sentence, the act of studying can be imagined as a continuous line (**imperfetto**), while Jim's call, in the present perfect (**passato prossimo**), is represented by the slash that interrupts the continuous line. The act of studying may have continued before and after the phone call.

Mentre **studiavo** (continuous)	Jim ha preparato la cena. (completed event)
While I was studying	*Jim prepared dinner.*

_____/_____

However, with both verbs in the **imperfetto**, the actions are simultaneous but incomplete and can be depicted as two parallel lines.

Mentre studiavo (continuous)	Jim ascoltava la musica. (continuous)
While I studied	*Jim listened to music.*

_____

_____

The **imperfetto** is also used with:

◆ References to the time of day, the weather, and age in the past

> **Erano** solo le 5.30 di mattina e **faceva** già caldo.
> *It was only 5:30 in the morning and it was already hot.*

◆ Descriptions of physical and psychological states of being

> Anna **era** una bambina molto vivace.
> *Anna was a very active child.*

> **Avevamo** paura delle grandi stanze buie.
> *We were afraid of the large dark rooms.*

The following words and phrases tend to trigger the **imperfetto**:

da piccolo	*as a child*
di solito	*usually*
sempre	*always*
generalmente	*generally*
ogni giorno, estate	*every day, summer, etc.*
mentre	*while*

Other words tend to trigger the **passato prossimo** because they imply a completed event:

un giorno	*one day*
una volta	*once*
dieci anni fa	*ten years ago*

Forms of the **imperfetto**

The **imperfetto** suffix is formed by the first letter of the infinitive ending (-*are*, -*ere*, or -*ire*) followed by the **imperfetto** suffixes, which, after that first vowel, are the same for all three conjugations.

amare		leggere		capire	
am**avo**	am**avamo**	legg**evo**	legg**evamo**	cap**ivo**	cap**ivamo**
am**avi**	am**avate**	legg**evi**	legg**evate**	cap**ivi**	cap**ivate**
am**ava**	am**avano**	legg**eva**	legg**evano**	cap**iva**	cap**ivano**

Most verbs are regular in the **imperfetto**—the few irregular verbs have the same stem as their irregular present tense, which then combines with the regular **imperfetto** suffixes as shown earlier.

INFINITIVE	PRESENT ROOT	IMPERFECT FIRST PERSON
bere	**bev**o	**bev**evo
dire	**dic**o	**dic**evo
fare	**fac**cio	**fac**evo (Note: only one **c**)

The **imperfetto** form of **avere** is regular, but **essere** is irregular, as shown here. Notice how each form begins with **er** and that the suffix endings are similar but not the same as the **-are** conjugation. Take care to memorize this auxiliary verb correctly. The most common problem generally occurs with the forms that have no **v**.

ero	eravamo
eri	eravate
era	erano

Nota bene

Besides those previously described, there are several other uses of the **imperfetto**, such as after **ho visto** or **ho sentito** with a relative clause.

Ho sentito un programma **che parlava** di economia.
I heard a program that talked about economics.

Ho visto gli studenti **che studiavano** per l'esame.
I saw the students who were studying for the exam.

The **imperfetto** is also used to ask questions politely.

Volevo farLe una domanda.
I wanted to ask you (formal) *a question.*

Ti telefonavo per chiederti un favore.
I was calling to ask you a favor.

Mi domandavo se . . .
I was wondering if . . .

Imperfect or present perfect?

The use of the imperfect or the present perfect often depends on the nuances and meaning a speaker wants to express. Both of the following sentences are correct, but the different tenses convey a slightly different meaning.

Sapevo che Marco non era felice.   **Ho saputo** che Marco non era felice
I knew Marco wasn't happy.   *I found out that Marco wasn't happy.*

Change the following verbs from the **presente** into the **imperfetto**.

ESEMPIO   parla   *parlava*

1. diciamo   _____

2. bevete   _____

3. fanno   _____

4. sei   _____

5. faccio   _____

6. prende   _____

7. vieni   _____

8. c'è   _____

9. andiamo   _____

10. (loro) sono   _____

Complete the sentences with the **imperfetto** or the **passato prossimo** of the given verb.

1. Da piccola io _____ (essere) molto timida.

2. Noi _____ (avere) un cane per molti anni.

3. _____ (fare) sempre caldo d'estate.

4. Di solito mia nonna _____ (andare) al mare.

5. Nell'estate del 2006 (io) _____ (vedere) la Tour Eiffel.

6. La casa _____ (sembrare) disabitata.

7. Charlie Chaplin _____ (fare) molti film.

8. Mio padre _____ (dire) sempre quello che _____ (pensare).

The past perfect (il trapassato prossimo)

The past perfect (**trapassato prossimo**) tense is used for activities that occurred before another activity in the past. This compound tense combines the auxiliary **avere** or **essere** in the imperfect tense with the past participle of the verb. Adverbs of frequency, such as **ancora** (*yet*), **già** (*already*), and **sempre** (*always*), are often used with this tense and are placed between the auxiliary and the participle.

Transitive verbs combine the auxiliary **avere** in the **imperfetto** + the past participle.

> A otto anni non **avevo** ancora **imparato** a nuotare.
> *At eight I **had not** yet **learned** how to swim.*

Intransitive verbs combine the auxiliary **essere** in the **imperfetto** + the past participle of the verb.

> Quando sono arrivata alla stazione di Milano, il treno per Como **era** già **partito**.
> *When I arrived at the Milan station, the train for Como **had already left**.*

ESERCIZIO 8·3

*Change the following verbs from the **presente** to the **trapassato prossimo**. Then check your auxiliaries and irregular participles with the list on pages 60–61.*

ESEMPIO   arrivano   *erano arrivati*

1. partono   _____

2. mangiate   _____

3. ritorna   _____

4. sei   _____

5. va   _____

6. prendete   _____

7. dice   _____

8. chiediamo _____

9. mettono   _____

10. studio   _____

Past absolute tense

The past absolute (**il passato remoto**), also called the historic past, is used for events that occurred long ago and have little connection to the present. The **passato prossimo** (or near past), instead, is used to describe an event that still has an effect on the present. However, in narrative texts such as biographies, opera librettos, novels, short stories, and children's books, the **passato remoto** is the preferred tense. As you read such texts you will immediately recognize verbs in this tense, since many of the stems are regular. The **passato remoto** is not used frequently in spoken Italian, but the recognition of verbs in this tense is important for those who will be reading in Italian.

The suffixes in the **passato remoto** are as follows:

-are	-ere	-ire
-ai	-ei *or* -etti	-ii
-asti	-esti	-isti
-ò	-è *or* -ette	-ì
-ammo	-emmo	-immo
-aste	-este	-iste
-arono	-erono *or* -ettero	-irono

Notice how the first letter of each suffix corresponds to the first letter of the infinitive with only one exception (-**ò** in the third person of -**are** verbs) and that the remaining letters of each suffix are the same for the three conjugations.

Irregular verbs

Here are the three most commonly used irregular verbs. Notice how the **essere** forms all start with the same letter **f**, and how both **dare** and **stare** change their roots to **de**- and **ste**-.

essere (*to be*)	dare (*to give*)	stare (*to be, to stay*)
fui	detti *or* diedi	stetti
fosti	desti	stesti
fu	dette *or* diede	stette
fummo	demmo	stemmo
foste	deste	steste
furono	dettero *or* diedero	stettero

1-3-3 verbs

There are some verbs that are irregular only in the first- and third-person singular and third-person plural, while the remaining persons follow the regular form.

vedere (*to see*)	
vidi	vedemmo
vedesti	vedeste
vide	**videro**

Notice how the root of the first person **vidi** occurs again in the third-person singular and plural. This is a very common pattern in the **passato remoto** tense.

Look at the infinitive and irregular first-person forms of common verbs that follow this 1-3-3 pattern and make a mental note of the patterns.

avere	→	ebbi	*I had*
bere	→	bevvi	*I drank*
cadere	→	caddi	*I fell*
chiedere	→	chiesi	*I asked*
conoscere	→	conobbi	*I met, knew*
dare	→	diedi *or* detti	*I gave*
decidere	→	decisi	*I decided*
dire	→	dissi	*I said*
fare	→	feci	*I did, made*
leggere	→	lessi	*I read*
mettere	→	misi	*I put*
nascere	→	nacqui	*I was born*
perdere	→	persi *or* perdetti	*I lost*
prendere	→	presi	*I took*
sapere	→	seppi	*I knew*
scegliere	→	scelsi	*I chose*
scendere	→	scesi	*I descended*
scrivere	→	scrissi	*I wrote*
vedere	→	vidi	*I saw*
venire	→	venni	*I came*
vincere	→	vinsi	*I won*
vivere	→	vissi	*I lived*
volere	→	volli	*I wanted*

Nota bene

Derivations of these words will have the same irregular participle. For example:

per**mettere**	→	per**misi**	*I allowed*
tras**mettere**	→	tras**misi**	*I transmitted*
inter**venire**	→	inter**venni**	*I intervened*

*Caesar is said to have announced after one of his conquests "**Veni, vidi, vici.**" These words are not so different from what you would say today in the **passato remoto**, as you will see by consulting the verbs listed earlier and completing the following Italian phrase:*

Cesare disse, "_____, _____, _____."

*Indicate the verbs in the **passato remoto** and provide the infinitive.*

ESEMPIO   Johann Sebastian Bach <u>nacque</u> nel 1685.   *nascere*

1. Silvio Pellico scrisse *le Mie Prigioni.* _____

2. Giuseppe Verdi compose *La Traviata.* _____

3. Michelangelo dipinse gli affreschi della Cappella Sistina. _____

4. Enrico Fermi e sua moglie si trasferirono a Chicago. _____

5. Vincenzo Bellini morì giovanissimo. _____

6. Sophia Loren fece molti film di successo. _____

7. Garibaldi vinse la battaglia di Milazzo nel 1860. _____

8. Elsa Morante visse a Roma. _____

9. I suoi genitori si conobbero nel 1968. _____

10. Mio nonno si sposò nel 1897. _____

Future and future perfect tenses

The future tense (**il futuro**) is used for actions that will take place in the future or may be taking place in the present (future of probability).

-are	-ere	-ire
parlerò	spenderò	dormirò
parlerai	spenderai	dormirai
parlerà	spenderà	dormirà
parleremo	spenderemo	dormiremo
parlerete	spenderete	dormirete
parleranno	spenderanno	dormiranno

Notice that the **-are** verbs change the **-a** of the infinitive to an **-e**, and that the suffixes are the same for all types of regular verbs. The first- and third-person singular is written with an accent on the final syllable in each conjugation.

The following words are commonly used with the **futuro**.

domani	*tomorrow*
dopodomani	*the day after tomorrow*
presto	*soon*
la settimana prossima	*next week*
il mese / l'anno prossimo	*next month / next year*
fra un anno	*in a year*
quando	*when*
appena	*as soon as*

The future of probability (**futuro di probabilità**) is used when speaking of an action that is possible or probable but not verified. It is used when making a guess or conjecture. This corresponds to the use of *must* in English.

Dove sono le tue chiavi?	*Where are your keys?*
Saranno vicino alla porta.	*They **must be** near the door.*

ESERCIZIO
10·1

*Change the following regular verbs from the **presente** into the **futuro**.*

1. parla _____

2. prendono _____

3. capite _____

4. arrivo   _____

5. leggiamo   _____

6. paga   _____

7. mangiate   _____

8. metto   _____

9. arriviamo   _____

10. dormono   _____

Irregular verbs in the future tense (il futuro)

There are some verbs that change their stems in the future tense but have the same suffixes as the regular **futuro**. The best way to learn these is to carefully notice how the infinitive and the irregular stems compare.

Here is a list of common irregular verbs with a short description of their patterns:

DROPS THE THIRD-TO-LAST LETTER OF THE INFINITIVE	DROPS THE THIRD- AND FOURTH-TO-LAST LETTER OF THE INFINITIVE AND DOUBLES THE **R**
avere → avr-	rimanere → rimarr-
andare →andr-	tenere → terr-
cadere →cadr-	venire → verr-
dovere →dovr-	volere → vorr-
potere → potr-	
vedere →vedr-	
vivere →vivr-	
sapere →sapr-	

The **futuro** of the verbs **essere**, **dare**, **fare**, and **stare** is slightly irregular and is another subgroup that follows the same pattern.

essere (*to be*)

sarò	saremo
sarai	sarete
sarà	saranno

dare → darò, etc.
fare → farò, etc.
stare → starò, etc.

Nota bene

A common idiomatic expression in the **futuro** includes:

Staremo a vedere!   *We shall see!*

Un proverbio

Se son rose fioriranno.   *If they are roses, then they will bloom.* (This means that if something has promise it will eventually prove itself. The English version of this proverb is "time will tell.")

*Change the following sentences from the **presente** to the **futuro**.*

1. Lavoro domani.

   _____

2. Quando arriva l'inverno, andiamo in Sicilia.

   _____

3. Domani comincia la scuola.

   _____

4. Tu e Giovanni tornate l'anno prossimo?

   _____

5. Stasera resto a casa.

   _____

6. La settimana prossima arriva mia sorella!

   _____

7. Non vuole andare al concerto.

   _____

8. Sei qui per la festa?

   _____

9. Cosa fa quando finisce l'università?

   _____

10. Devo trovare un lavoro.

   _____

The future perfect tense (il futuro anteriore)

The future perfect (**il futuro anteriore**) is used to express an action in the future that will have already occurred by the time a second action takes place. It specifies which of two actions in the future happened first. In English, the present or future is often used, and which action precedes the other is understood through logic or context rather than a specific verb tense.

> Quando avrò ventun'anni **mi sarò laureato.**
> *When I am twenty-one, **I will have graduated**.*

Since the **futuro anteriore** is unusual in English, most native English speakers would simply say:

> Quando avrò ventun'anni, **mi laureerò.**
> *When I am twenty-one, **I will graduate**.*

The sentence using the **futuro anteriore** means:

*When I turn twenty-one (**futuro**), I will have <u>already</u> graduated (**futuro anteriore**).*

In the second example, the graduation occurs during the twenty-first year, while in the first example, the graduation will have already occurred by the twenty-first year. The second example is simpler, and in most cases is perfectly adequate to communicate an action in the future.

The **futuro anteriore** can also express a past action that is likely to have occurred. In English this can be expressed with *must have* + verb.

Dove sono andati Roberto e Paolo?	*Where did Roberto and Paolo go?*
Saranno andati al cinema.	***They must have gone** to the movies.*

ESERCIZIO
10·3

*Translate the following sentences into Italian, using the **futuro di probabilità**. When referring to a possibility in the present, use the **futuro** of the main verb. When referring to a possibility that may have already occurred, use the **futuro anteriore**.*

ESEMPIO   *They must be happy to be in Rome.*   <u>Saranno contenti di essere a Roma.</u>

They probably missed the train.   <u>Avranno perso il treno.</u>

1. *Maria must be happy with her new job.*

   _____

2. *You probably met a lot of interesting people.* (**la gente**, singular)

   _____

3. *I must have left my book on the train.*

   _____

4. *The student must have missed the bus.*

   _____

5. *We must have seen a hundred films!*

   _____

6. *The Italian team must have won the game.*

   _____

7. *She probably has a lot of questions.*

   _____

8. *He'll probably be back by 8:00.*

   _____

9. *How much could I have slept?*

   _____

10. *How much do you think it costs?*

   _____

Present and perfect conditional tenses

In English the conditional is constructed with the auxiliary *would* + verb, while in Italian it is a separate tense. **Vorrei** is probably the most frequently used conditional verb, and it is used to make polite requests. In Italian the conditional has a present form (one word) and a past form (two words).

The present conditional (il condizionale)

The present conditional (**condizionale**) is used to express a wish, to give advice, and to make polite requests or suppositions. As with the **futuro**, the first letter of the –**are** ending changes to an -**e**, and the six suffixes are the same for all regular and irregular -**are**, -**ere**, and -**ire** verbs.

-are	-ere	-ire
parlerei	spenderei	dormirei
parleresti	spenderesti	dormiresti
parlerebbe	spenderebbe	dormirebbe
parleremmo	spenderemmo	dormiremmo
parlereste	spendereste	dormireste
parlerebbero	spenderebbero	dormirebbero

Study tip

When learning a new tense, look carefully at the patterns of the suffixes, noticing the details that distinguish it from other tenses. In the conditional, for example, the first person does not end in an -**o** (as it does in the present, imperfect, and future); the suffixes all start with the letter -**e**, and the third person singular and plural forms contain a double **b**. The patterns you notice yourself will help you anchor each tense in your memory, making them easier to retrieve and use automatically and without stopping to think as you speak.

Irregular verbs in the conditional

There are many verbs that change their stem in the **condizionale** and then combine with the regular suffix endings. The best way to learn these is to carefully notice how the infinitive and the irregular stem compare. Also remember that the **futuro** and the **condizionale** share the same irregular verbs.

Here is a list of the common irregular verbs in the **condizionale**, divided according to their distinctive patterns.

DROPS THE THIRD-TO-LAST LETTER OF THE INFINITIVE	DROPS THE THIRD- AND FOURTH-TO-LAST LETTER OF THE INFINITIVE AND DOUBLES THE **R**
avere → avr-	rimanere → rimarr-
andare → andr-	tenere → terr-
cadere → cadr-	venire → verr-
dovere → dovr-	volere → vorr-
potere → potr-	
vedere → vedr-	
vivere → vivr-	
sapere → sapr-	

The verbs **essere**, **dare**, **fare**, and **stare** are another set of verbs that share a distinctive pattern. **Dare**, **fare**, and **stare** do *not* change the infinitive ending -**a** to an -**e**.

essere → **sa** + suffix	
sarei	saremmo
saresti	sareste
sarebbe	sarebbero

dare → darei, etc.
fare → farei, etc.
stare → starei, etc.

Idiomatic expressions in the conditional

Come **sarebbe** a dire?
What do you mean? What are you talking about?

Ti **andrebbe** di andare al cinema?
How would you feel about going to the movies?

Faresti meglio a studiare un po' di più.
You would be better off studying a little more.

ESERCIZIO
11·1

*Change the following sentences from the **presente** to the **condizionale**.*

1. Voglio un bicchiere di acqua minerale per favore.

_____

2. Va a studiare.

_____

3. Andiamo in Francia.

_____

4. È facile.

_____

5. Vogliamo andare in vacanza.

_____

6. Sono contenti. (third person plural)

_____

7. Partite subito?

_____

8. Vai in Canada?

_____

9. Non faccio niente.

_____

10. Quando torni?

_____

The perfect conditional (**il condizionale passato**)

The perfect conditional (**condizionale passato**) is used for actions that would, could, or should have occurred in the past. It combines the auxiliary **avere** or **essere** in the **condizionale** + the participle of the verb.

> **Avrei telefonato** ma non avevo il tuo numero.
> *I would have called (you) but I didn't have your number.*

> **Avrebbero comprato** una casa più spaziosa.
> *They would have bought a more spacious home.*

> **Sarei arrivata** prima ma ho perso il treno.
> *I would have arrived earlier but I missed the train.*

To express *should have* + past or *could have* + past use the **condizionale passato** of **dovere** (*should*) and **potere** (*could*). The auxiliary of the main verb should be used to form compound tenses, although this distinction is not always made in common informal speech.

> **Avrei dovuto** telefonare.   *I should have phoned.*
> **Sarei dovuto/a** andare.   *I should have gone.*
> **Avrei potuto** vincere.   *I could have won.*
> **Sarei potuto/a** arrivare prima.   *I could have arrived earlier.*

For each phrase in column 1, choose the letter of the most logical conclusion from column 2.

1. Sarei andato al cinema _____

2. Avremmo mangiato una pizza _____

3. Avrei comprato una BMW _____

4. Ti saresti divertita alla festa _____

5. Sarebbero stati felici insieme _____

6. Avrebbe potuto vincere _____

7. Ti avrei telefonato _____

8. Avremmo voluto avvertirti _____

9. Ti avrei salutato _____

a. ma non ti ho riconosciuto.

b. ma non avevamo il cellulare.

c. ma non avevo il tuo numero.

d. ma era troppo distratto.

e. ma lui era troppo geloso.

f. ma il film era già cominciato.

g. ma la pizzeria era già chiusa.

h. ma costava troppo.

i. ma sei arrivata troppo tardi.

*Choose the appropriate verb from the following list and change it to the **condizionale passato** to complete each sentence. There are two extra verbs.*

andare	dovere	fare	vendere	cambiare
essere	avere	volere	rimanere	studiare

1. Stefania _____ economia ma non è molto brava in matematica.

2. Cameriere, _____ un caffè macchiato, per favore.

3. Giovanni _____ colazione al bar dietro casa, ma oggi è chiuso.

4. Io _____ al mercato, ma ormai è troppo tardi.

5. I miei amici _____ casa, ma si trovano bene in quel quartiere.

6. Senti, Marco, _____ studiare di più se vuoi superare il corso.

7. Scusi, _____ da cambiare 100 euro?

8. Tu e Valentina _____ liberi sabato sera per una cena da noi?

*Make the following sentences more polite by using the **condizionale** without changing the register (formal/informal).*

1. Mi dai una mano?

   _____

2. Mi fa lo sconto, signora?

   _____

3. Dottore, mi dà un appuntamento per domani?

   _____

4. Signori, possono tornare domani?

   _____

5. Marco, puoi chiamarmi domani?

   _____

6. Vieni con me in Italia?

   _____

7. Professore, è possibile rimandare l'esame fino a domani?

   _____

8. Può ripetere la domanda, per favore?

   _____

The subjunctive

·12·

The subjunctive construction is not used much any more in English, but in Italian it is used frequently in academic, political, or formal situations. There are certain phrases and words that trigger the use of the subjunctive and can easily be avoided by speakers who do not wish to use it until they are ready.

The subjunctive (il congiuntivo) with subordinate clauses

The subjunctive (**congiuntivo**) is used in subordinate clauses that express emotion, judgment, necessity, opinion, possibility, wishes, doubt, or an action that has not occurred. The independent clause is identifiable as a clause that can stand on its own. Here are some verbs and expressions that trigger, or make necessary, the use of the **congiuntivo**.

INDEPENDENT CLAUSE	SUBORDINATE CLAUSE
Penso	che Roberto **suoni** in un'orchestra.
I think	*that Roberto **plays** in an orchestra.*
Spero	che gli amici non **facciano** tardi.
I hope	*that my friends **are** not **late**.*
Sembra	che il tempo **migliori**.
It seems	*that the weather **is improving**.*
Dubito	che Gina **arrivi** puntuale.
I doubt	*that Gina **will be arriving** on time.*
Credo	che gli studenti **debbano** prima dare un esame.
I believe	*that the students **must** first take an exam.*
Temo	che Gianni **perda** il lavoro.
I fear	*that Gianni **will lose** his job.*
Ho paura	che il regalo non gli **piaccia**.
I am afraid	*that she doesn't **like** the gift.*

All the verbs in the independent clause indicate uncertainty, emotion, opinion, or doubt. The subordinate clause is always introduced by **che**, with the verb that follows in the **congiuntivo**.

The following expressions also trigger the subjunctive:

sebbene	*although*
purché	*as long as*
a condizione che	*provided that*
a meno che non	*unless*
senza che	*without*
è possibile che	*it is possible that*
è probabile che	*it is probable that*
senza che	*without + verb*
prima che	*before + verb*

Important: If the main clause uses a verb that expresses *certainty*, then the indicative is used. Here are some verbs that use the indicative rather than the **congiuntivo**.

So che il treno parte alle 3.00.	*I know the train is departing at 3:00.*
È certo che arriva domani.	*It is certain that he is arriving tomorrow.*
Ricordo che ha una casa molto bella.	*I remember that he has a beautiful home.*
È vero che torna stasera?	*Is it true that he's returning tonight?*
Dicono tutti che beve troppo.	*Everyone says he drinks too much.*

The four subjunctive tenses are present (**presente**), past (**passato**), imperfect (**imperfetto**), and past perfect (**trapassato**).

The present subjunctive is used after a main clause in the present tense if the action of both clauses occurs at the same time.

Penso che Luca **canti** molto bene.	*I think Luca sings very well.*

The first, second, and third person of the present subjunctive are identical, ending in -**i** for -**are** verbs and in -**a** for -**ere** and -**ire** verbs. As a result of the three identical forms, the subject pronoun can be added for clarity if the subject is not already in the sentence.

Penso che **lui** canti molto bene.	*I think he sings very well.*

As you can see, the stems used in the present subjunctive are the same as those used in the present indicative.

-are	-ere	-ire
parli	spenda	dorma
parli	spenda	dorma
parli	spenda	dorma
parliamo	spendiamo	dormiamo
parliate	spendiate	dormiate
parlino	spendano	dormano

Indicate the correct form of the present subjunctive in each sentence, and then translate the sentences into English.

1. Credo che Mara (parli / parla) il francese.

2. Penso che Letizia (insegni / insegno) l'inglese.

3. Dubito che Eleonora mi (chiede / chieda) scusa.

4. Non è possibile che tu (dici / dica) sempre le bugie (*lies*)!

5. Sebbene Maria (guadagni / guadagna) molto, è sempre senza soldi.

6. Credo che quel ragazzo si (chiama / chiami) Andrea.

7. Penso che Gaia e Jim (vedono / vedano) molti film francesi.

8. Voglio parlarti prima che tu (decidi / decida) di lasciare il lavoro.

9. Sembra che Sandro (parla / parli) spesso di te.

10. Non voglio che (pagate / paghiate) sempre voi!

Present subjunctive of irregular verbs

The three irregular verbs **essere**, **dare**, and **stare** have similar forms in the present subjunctive, so they are more easily learned together. As with the regular present subjunctive verbs, the first-, second-, and third-person singular are the same.

essere	dare	stare
sia	**dia**	**stia**
siamo	diamo	stiamo
siate	diate	stiate
siano	diano	stiano

Avere and **andare** are also irregular in the present subjunctive and, as all verbs in this tense, the first three persons are the same. Notice how the subjunctive of **andare** and **capire** use the same stems as the present indicative. This similarity with the present indicative also applies to **-isc** verbs, which omit it in the first- and second-person plural.

avere	andare	capire
abbia	vada	capisca
abbiamo	andiamo	capiamo
abbiate	andiate	capiate
abbiano	vadano	capiscano

ESERCIZIO
12·2

Complete the chart with the missing forms of the present subjunctive.

ESSERE	AVERE	PARLARE	PRENDERE	FINIRE
sia	_____	_____	_____	finisca
_____	abbiamo	_____	_____	_____
_____	_____	parliate	_____	_____
_____	_____	_____	prendano	_____

The past subjunctive

If the action of the subordinate clause has taken place *before* the action of the independent clause, the past subjunctive will be used. In both sentences below, the subordinate clause describes an event that has already occurred.

Penso che Lucia **sia andata** a Roma.   (Remember the agreement!)
*I think Lucia **has gone** to Rome.*

Penso che Paolo **abbia fatto** l'esame.
*I think Paolo **took** the exam.*

Similar to other compound tenses, the past subjunctive combines the present subjunctive of **avere** (if transitive) or of **essere** (if intransitive), followed by the past participle of the verb. As always, with **essere**, the participle agrees with the subject in gender and number.

The imperfect subjunctive (**congiuntivo imperfetto**) is used when the main clause is not in the present, but in the past, imperfect, or conditional tenses. Look at the regular forms below and notice how all the suffixes after the -**a**, -**e**, or -**i** of the stem are the same for the three conjugations (-**ssi**, -**sse**, -**ssimo**, -**ste**, -**ssero**). The stress of the **congiuntivo imperfetto** always falls on the -**a**, -**e**, or -**i** before the suffix.

-are	-ere	-ire
parlassi	spendessi	dormissi
parlassi	spendessi	dormissi
parlasse	spendesse	dormisse
parlassimo	spendessimo	dormissimo
parlaste	spendeste	dormiste
parlassero	spendessero	dormissero

The auxiliaries avere and essere

Avere is regular and essere is irregular in the imperfect subjunctive. Notice how the irregular stem fo- is combined with the congiuntivo imperfetto endings -ssi, -sse, -ssimo, -ste, -ssero. Verbs such as bere, dire, and fare (with only one c) use the same stem as in the present indicative.

essere	
fossi	fossimo
fossi	foste
fosse	fossero

The past perfect (or pluperfect) subjunctive (il congiuntivo trapassato)

This is formed with the congiuntivo imperfetto of the auxiliary verbs essere (if intransitive) or avere (if transitive) and the past participle of the verb. It is used in subordinate clauses following the independent clause in the imperfect indicative (l'imperfetto), conditional (il condizionale), or any past tense. Since the first- and second-person singular forms are identical, there are only five forms to learn.

(io, tu)	avessi parlato	avessi veduto	avessi capito
(lui/lei, Lei)	avesse parlato	avesse veduto	avesse capito
(noi)	avessimo parlato	avessimo veduto	avessimo capito
(voi)	aveste parlato	aveste veduto	aveste capito
(loro)	avessero parlato	avessero veduto	avessero capito

As always, the intransitive verbs andare, essere, venire, tornare, etc. use the auxiliary essere and the participle ending agrees with subject in gender and number.

(io, tu)	fossi andato/a
(lui/lei, Lei)	fosse andato/a
(noi)	fossimo andati/e
(voi)	foste andati/e
(loro)	fossero andati/e

When the main clause is in the conditional or any past tense, the following subordinate clause must be either in the imperfetto or congiuntivo trapassato. The chart that follows will clarify the relationship between the two clauses.

MAIN CLAUSE	SUBORDINATE CLAUSE	TENSE
present, future, imperative	same time	present subjunctive
	already occurred	past subjunctive
past tense, imperfect, conditional	same time	imperfect subjunctive
	already occurred	past perfect subjunctive

In English, the subjunctive is often used with the verb *to wish*, and the time relationship (whether or not the action of the subordinate clause is simultaneous or has already occurred) is also expressed. The following chart illustrates the time relationship between the two clauses. The base sentences in English are:

INDEPENDENT CLAUSE	SUBORDINATE CLAUSE
I wish	*that Roberto **were** in Rome.*
I wish	*that Roberto **had been** in Rome.*
I wished	*that Roberto **were** in Rome.*
I wished	*that Roberto **had been** in Rome.*

Now let us look at the Italian version of a similar sentence:

INDEPENDENT CLAUSE	SUBORDINATE CLAUSE	TENSE
Penso	che Roberto **sia** a Roma.	C. presente (*present subjunctive*)
	che Roberto **sia stato** a Roma.	C. passato (*past subjunctive*)
Pensavo	che Roberto **fosse** a Roma.	C. imperfetto (*imperfect subjunctive*)
	che Roberto **fosse stato** a Roma.	C. trapassato (*past perfect subjunctive*)

Nota bene

Remember that if the action in the two clauses is simultaneous, the subordinate clause *will not* include the past participle. When expressing a prior action, the subordinate clause will include the past participle. There are often other clue words in the sentence that will indicate whether the action has already occurred (**già** *already*), time references such as **la settimana**, **il mese**, **l'anno scorso**, **stamattina**, **ieri** (*last week, last month, last year, this morning, yesterday*) or has yet to occur (**domani, la settimana, il mese, l'anno prossimo** *tomorrow, next week, next month, next year*).

Also remember that if the main clause expresses certainty (*I know, I was told, I am sure,* etc.), the subjunctive mood is not to be used.

ESERCIZIO 12·3

Complete the sentences with the appropriate verbs. Some sentences state a fact and will use the indicative.

1. Pensavo che Riccardo Muti _____ (venire) a Chicago l'anno scorso.

2. Mi hanno detto che (tu) _____ (partire) presto stamattina.

3. Tutti sanno che _____ (vincere) la Roma.

4. Speravo che _____ (vincere) i Cubs (plurale).

5. Sai che Nina _____ (partire) domani?

6. Vorrei che mi (loro) _____ (dire) tutto.

7. Pensi che loro _____ (andare) in l'Italia l'anno scorso?

8. Pensavo che l'università _____ (essere) più difficile.

9. Ho paura che domani _____ (piovere).

10. Non immaginavo che tu _____ (avere) paura di volare.

The imperative

13

The imperative (**imperativo**) is most commonly used to make a suggestion or to give advice and to issue a warning or a command. An imperative sentence is often written with an exclamation point and may consist of only one word. It is common to add **per favore**, **per piacere**, or **per cortesia**, all of which mean *please*, to make the command more courteous.

The following chart illustrates the imperative forms. Notice that the imperative is never use in the first-person singular.

(tu)	Guarda!	Prendi!	Senti!
(Lei, *formal*)	Guardi!	Prenda!	Senta!
(noi)	Guardiamo!	Prendiamo!	Sentiamo!
(voi)	Guardate!	Prendete!	Sentite!
(loro)*	Guardino!	Prendano!	Sentano!

---

*The use of the third-person plural formal is rare in current Italian. The **voi** form is preferred.

When using the **imperativo** with a direct- or indirect-object pronoun, it attaches to the end of the verb in all cases *except* for the formal, where it precedes the verb.

> Prendi i libri! → Prend**ili**!
> *Take the books! → Take them!*

but

> Signorina, prenda i libri! → **Li** prenda!

The negative imperative (**imperativo negativo**) in the **tu** form is very simple. **Non** precedes the infinitive form of the verb.

> Non fumare! *Don't smoke!*

In all other persons, the negative is expressed by placing **non** before the conjugated verb.

> Non partiamo domani, partiamo oggi! — *Let's not leave tomorrow, let's leave today!*
> Vi prego, non lasciate la cucina in disordine! — *I'm begging you, don't leave the kitchen in a mess!*

Nota bene

Common idioms that use the imperative:

IDIOMATIC PHRASE	
Non mi seccare!	*Don't bother me!*
Non ci provare!	*Don't you dare!*

ESERCIZIO
13·1

*A friend is having a dinner party and needs your advice. Use the **imperativo** to make suggestions, with direct-object pronouns whenever necessary.*

1. Posso invitare il tuo ex? Per favore, non _____!

2. Che cosa preparo da mangiare? _____ gli spaghetti alla carbonara!

3. Chi posso invitare? _____ Marco ed Elena!

4. Che cosa mi metto? _____ il tuo vestito nero!

5. Cosa dico al mio compagno di stanza? _____ di venire anche lui!

6. Quando faccio i compiti? _____ domani mattina!

7. Faccio anche una torta alla cioccolata? Sì, _____!

8. Beviamo lo champagne? Sì, _____!

ESERCIZIO
13·2

*Change the following verbs from the informal to the formal **imperativo**.*

1. Prendi il telefono! _____

2. Compra il latte! _____

3. Non tornare tardi! _____

4. Salutate i nostri amici! _____

5. Non ti preoccupare! _____

6. Fa' pure! _____

7. Entra! _____

8. Torna presto a trovarmi! _____

9. Accomodati! _____

10. Calmati! _____

PRACTICE MAKES PERFECT   Italian Problem Solver

13·3

*Using the informal **imperativo**, make these suggestions to a friend.*

1. *Let's have a party!* _____

2. *Don't eat all the pizza!* _____

3. *Come back!* _____

4. *Let's study together!* _____

5. *Call your mother!* _____

6. *Close the door!* _____

7. *Open the window!* _____

8. *Be careful!* _____

9. *Don't be late!* _____

10. *Write soon!* _____

13·4

*Suggest to your Italian professor the following, using the formal **imperativo**.*

1. *Please speak more slowly.*

   _____

2. *Please repeat the question.*

   _____

3. *Please give me two more days.*

   _____

4. *Please be patient!* (**avere pazienza**)

   _____

5. *Please don't get angry with the students.*

   _____

6. *Please speak a little louder.*

   _____

7. *Please open the window.*

   _____

8. *Please show us that movie.*

_____

9. *Please don't smoke in class!*

_____

10. *Please answer our messages!*

_____

The passive voice

14

A sentence is said to be in the active voice when the subject performs the action, and is in the passive voice when the subject receives the action of the verb. When a sentence is changed from the active voice to the passive voice, the subject and object change roles—the object becomes the agent, or doer. In Italian, the agent is preceded by **da** + article. In the passive voice, the agent may be omitted (see the third example).

ACTIVE VOICE	PASSIVE VOICE
1. Gli italiani **amano** la musica.	La musica **è amata** dagli italiani.
SUBJECT VERB OBJECT	SUBJECT VERB AGENT
2. I Romani **hanno costruito** il Colosseo.	Il Colosseo **è stato costruito** dai Romani.
SUBJECT VERB OBJECT	SUBJECT VERB AGENT
3. Mozart **ha composto** le più belle opere.	Le più belle opere **sono state composte**
SUBJECT VERB OBJECT	SUBJECT VERB
	da Mozart.
	AGENT

The active verb is made passive by changing the auxiliary verb from **avere** to **essere** and adding the participle of the main verb. When the active verb is in a compound tense (**passato prossimo, future anteriore, condizionale passato,** etc.), the participle **stato** is added in the passive voice: **essere** + **stato** + participle of the main verb. The participles must agree in gender and number with the subject. Notice in the following examples that the auxiliary verb **essere** will always be in the *same* tense as the active verb, followed by the participle of the base verb. The passive verb phrase of compound tenses will always have one more verb than the active form and will end with the two-word pattern of **stato** + participle of the main verb.

TENSE	ACTIVE VOICE	PASSIVE VOICE
presente	costruisce	è costruito/a
futuro	costruirà	**sarà** costruito
imperfetto	costruiva	**era** costruito
passato prossimo	ha costruito	**è stato** costruito
condizionale presente	costruirebbe	**sarebbe** costruito
condizionale passato	avrebbe costruito	**sarebbe stato** costruito
gerundio	essendo costruito	**essendo stato** costruito

Other passive auxiliaries

Although passive sentences as a rule use **essere** as the auxiliary:

♦ **venire** is used to emphasize the process of the action.

Il portone del convento **veniva chiuso** ogni sera alle 23.00.
*The front gate of the convent **was (got) closed** at 11:00 P.M.*

♦ **andare** + past participle is used to indicate necessity or obligation.

La pasta **va cotta** al dente.	*Pasta should (**is to be**) cooked al dente.*
Il letto **va fatto** tutti i giorni.	*The bed should be (**is to be made**) every day.*
Questa medicina **va presa** con i pasti.	*This medication **is to be taken** with meals.*

The following common expressions emphasize *what* should be done rather than *who* should be doing it.

va detto che	*it should be said that*
va ricordato che	*it should be remembered that*
va notato che	*it should be noted*
non va dimenticato che	*it should not be forgotten*

ESERCIZIO
14·1

Change the following sentences from the active voice to the passive voice as in the example.

1. Il baritono americano ha vinto il concorso.

   Il concorso è stato vinto dal baritono americano.

2. Elsa Morante ha scritto l'*Isola di Arturo*.

   _____

3. Avranno girato quel film a Cinecittà.

   _____

4. La squadra del Cameroon avrà vinto la partita.

   _____

5. Marco e Paola porteranno il vino rosso.

   _____

6. Roberto ha piantato i fiori.

   _____

7. Il governo approverà le nuove leggi.

   _____

8. Quel professore correggeva i temi in italiano.

   _____

9. I ragazzi avranno finito la torta.

_____

10. Il soprano ha cantato l'aria di *Aida*.

_____

The passive si (il si passivante)

Another passive construction uses the particle **si** with the active form of the verb in the third-person singular or plural depending on the subject. Remember that the passive voice can be used only with transitive verbs and that the subject usually follows the verb. This construction is preferable when the agent (or doer) is not expressed. With compound tenses, **essere** is used and the participle agrees with the subject in gender and number.

Non **si** è visto nessuno.	**Si** sono vendut**i** molti libri in questi giorni?
No one was seen.	*Were many books sold in the last few days?*
Si insegna bene l'italiano qui.	Dove **si** trovano i tartufi?
Italian is taught well here.	*Where are truffles found?*

ESERCIZIO
14·2

*Change the sentences using the **si passivante** form, which will begin each sentence, as in the example. Remember that (a) the **si passivante** sentence will always have one more verb than the passive voice and (b) the **si passivante** will never include the agent, or doer.*

1. La cena è stata preparata da Mario.

   Si è preparata la cena. _____

2. La camera verrà pulita dalla cameriera.

   _____

3. L'offerta è stata accettata da mio padre.

   _____

4. La casa è stata restaurata da un architetto famoso.

   _____

5. Quel libro è consigliato da Giuseppe.

   _____

6. Sono accettate carte di credito.

   _____

7. I quadri di Warhol sono stati venduti dal suo agente.

   _____

8. Le sue opere non sono mai state pubblicate da Einaudi.

_____

9. La mozzarella buona non è venduta al supermercato.

_____

10. I suoi documentari sono stati scelti dalla giuria.

_____

The impersonal si (il si impersonale)

The impersonal **si** is not the same as the passive **si** form, and the distinction is confusing even to native speakers. There are three important differences between the **si passivante** and the **si impersonale** constructions.

1. The **si passivante** can be used only with transitive verbs, since the object becomes the subject.

2. The **si impersonale** can be used with both transitive and intransitive verbs.

3. The **si impersonale** is always expressed in the third person.

Si cenava sempre dopo le 20.00.	A che ora **si arriva** a Napoli?
One (We) always ate dinner after 8 P.M.	_At what time will one (we) arrive in Rome?_

In the preceding examples, the verb does not have a specific subject but rather a general or impersonal one. It is used in giving instructions and directions and in public notices. In the sentences above, the subject could be _we, everyone, they, people._ The **si impersonale** is used to express this in a simpler and more elegant way.

There are two rules to remember when using the **si impersonale** in Italian:

1. Even though the verb is in the third-person singular, adjectives or nouns that refer to the subject must be in the plural.

    È meglio non mangiare quando **si è nervosi**.
    It is better not to eat when one is nervous.

    Quando si è **giovani**, non si pensa troppo al futuro.
    When you are young, you don't think too much about the future.

2. With the **si impersonale** compound tenses, always use **essere**. If the auxiliary of the verb is **avere**, the participle will end in **-o**.

Abbiamo deciso.	→	Si è decis**o**.
We decided.	→	_It was decided._
Abbiamo parlato molto ieri sera.	→	Si è parlat**o** molto ieri sera.
We spoke a lot last night.	→	_closest translation in English: A lot was said last night._

If the auxiliary is **essere**, the ending of the participle will be **-i**.

Siamo partiti.	→	Si è partit**i**.
Siamo tornati molto tardi.	→	Si è tornat**i** molto tardi.

Nota bene

When a reflexive verb, which uses **si** in the third person, is being used in the impersonal construction, it is not possible to use the impersonal **si** pronoun followed by the refexive **si** before a verb. The two **si**'s in a row would sound strange and confusing. This problem is solved by changing the first **si** to **ci**. The auxiliary is **essere**, and as we noted earlier, the participle is plural.

Ci si sveglia presto a casa mia.	*One gets up early at my house.*
Ci si è svegliati alle 5.30 stamattina.	*Everyone got up at 5:30 this morning.*

Proverbi

A caval donato **non si guarda** in bocca.
One doesn't look a gift horse in the mouth.

Sbagliando **s'impara.**
By making mistakes one learns.

ESERCIZIO
14·3

*Change the following sentences to the **si impersonale** form. Remember to use only the third-person singular.*

1. Bevono troppo la sera.

_____

2. Guadagnano poco da McDonald's.

_____

3. Parlano italiano in questo negozio?

_____

4. Non facciamo così.

_____

5. Vivono bene in Italia?

_____

6. Viaggiamo bene in treno.

_____

7. Oggi entriamo gratis alla Galleria Borghese.

_____

8. Dalla finestra vedevamo il mare.

_____

*Identify the following sentences as either **si impersonale (I)** or **si passivante (P)**.*

1. In quella regione si parla italiano e tedesco.   I   P

2. Con i miei genitori non si può parlare di politica.   I   P

3. Si può costruire una casa in poco più di un anno.   I   P

4. Dove si comprano i biglietti per l'autobus?   I   P

5. In quel ristorante si mangia bene e si spende poco!   I   P

6. In che mese si raccolgono le olive?   I   P

7. Ci si diverte sempre a casa di Marco.   I   P

8. Si deve studiare molto per imparare una lingua straniera.   I   P

*Change the following sentences from the **presente** to the **passato prossimo**, making all necessary adjustments (auxiliary, adjective, and participle agreement).*

1. Si parte alle 10.00.

_____

2. Si trova il gatto?

_____

3. Ci si sveglia tardi stamattina.

_____

4. La vendemmia si fa in ottobre?

_____

5. Si torna dalla Sardegna in luglio.

_____

6. L'insalata non si mangia come antipasto.

_____

7. Si vedono più stelle nel deserto?

_____

8. Si arriva presto in metropolitana.

_____

Prepositions

15

Prepositions are words placed before (pre-posed) words or phrases to show how they are related. In Italian there are simple prepositions (one word) and combined prepositions (preposition + article).

> Sono andata **al** cinema **con** le mie amiche **in** bicicletta.
> *I went **to** the movies **with** my friends **on** my bike.*

Simple prepositions

Simple prepositions clarify the relationship between two elements in a phrase. There are eight simple prepositions:

a
su
da
di
in
per
con
tra / fra

The first five, when followed by a definite article, combine with the article to form combined prepositions. We will look first at how and when simple prepositions are used.

Most prepositions have several meanings and their use differs from one language to another. Learning them in the context of small phrases will help you use them fluently and correctly.

The preposition a

The preposition **a** is used:

- before an indirect object

dare **a** Cesare	scrivere **a** Roberto
to give to Caesar	*to write to Roberto*

- after verbs indicating being or movement toward or within places

Abito **a** Roma.	Andiamo **a** Napoli.	Quando arrivate **a** Venezia?
I live in Rome.	*Let's go to Naples.*	*When are you arriving in Venice?*

◆ to link the conjugated verb *to go* with an infinitive verb

Oggi Mario non va **a** lavorare.   Andiamo **a** vedere Mamma Roma!
Today Mario is not going to work.   *Let's go see Mamma Roma!*

Nota bene

When the preposition **a** is followed by a vowel, it may be changed to **ad**, especially when that vowel is an –a, so as to make both **a**'s audible. This is optional, but in central and northern Italy it is still preferred.

Lavoro **ad** Ancona.   Hanno telefonato **ad** Alessandra.

The preposition con

The preposition **con** is used to combine elements in a phrase, just as *with* is used in English.

Prendo il gelato **con** le fragole.   Andiamo al mare **con** Isabella.
I'll take the ice cream with strawberries.   *We're going to the beach with Isabella.*

The preposition da

The preposition **da** is used:

◆ to express movement away from or distance from a place

Il treno parte **da** Roma alle 2.00.   *The train is leaving from Rome at 2:00.*
Abito a un chilometro **da** Firenze.   *I live a kilometer away from Florence.*

◆ with verbs in the present tense to indicate an amount of time from the past to the present

Abito a Roma **da** cinque anni.   *I have been living in Rome for five years.*

◆ with a proper name, meaning *at*, to indicate a restaurant or someone's home

da Giordano   **da** Cipriani   **da** mamma
Giordano's   *Cipriani's*   *to mom's house*

◆ with articles of clothing to describe their particular use

scarpe **da** tennis   tuta **da** ginnastica   costume **da** bagno
tennis shoes   *gym clothes*   *swimsuit*

◆ with **niente** or **qualcosa** + infinitive

niente **da** fare   qualcosa **da** mangiare
nothing to do   *something to eat*

The preposition di

The preposition **di** is used:

◆ to indicate possession and city of origin

il libro **di** Davide   la voce **di** mia madre
David's book   *my mother's voice*

Sono **di** Roma.
I am from Rome.

- with a specific quantity (after the container, volume, weight, etc.)

  una bottiglia **di** vino bianco   un litro **di** latte
  a bottle of white wine   *a liter of milk*

- for quantities of a million or billion

  un milione **di** euro   un miliardo **di** anni fa
  a million euros   *a billion years ago*

- to describe what something is made of (a material or fabric)

  un vestito **di** lino   un cucchiaio **d'**argento   una giacca **di** pelle
  a linen dress   *a silver spoon*   *a leather jacket*

The preposition **in**

The preposition **in** is used before a country, region, continent, rooms of the house, street names, piazzas, means of transportation, seasons, and months and to indicate institutional buildings.

in Francia	in Toscana	in Europa
in France	*in Tuscany*	*in Europe*

in giugno	in estate	in cucina
in June	*in the summer*	*in the kitchen*

The preposition **per**

The preposition **per** is used to express purpose or function.

Sono in Italia **per** studiare la musica.   Usiamo la macchina **per** viaggiare.
I am in Italy to study music.   *We use the car to travel.*

The preposition **su**

The preposition **su** is generally used in reference to a location, as in English.

Vorrei abitare **su** un isola.   Ho messo le foto **su** Facebook.
I want to live on an island.   *I put the pictures on Facebook.*

The prepositions **tra / fra**

The prepositions **tra / fra** are interchangeable and mean *between* when indicating location or a time in the future.

La banca è **tra** la libreria e il supermercato.
The bank is between the bookstore and the supermarket.

Arrivo **fra** due ore.
I'll be arriving in two hours.

Proverbio

Tra il dire e il fare c'è di mezzo il mare.
Between saying and doing there is the sea.

What is the closest English version of this proverb?

Match the phrases with the most logical prepositional phrases to complete each sentence.

1. Ogni estate vado _____   a. per studiare architettura.

2. Lavoro a Roma, ma abito _____   b. tra il ristorante e la libreria.

3. Ieri sera sono tornato _____   c. di Roberto.

4. Questo libri sono _____   d. a Firenze.

5. Il mio ufficio è _____   e. in Italia per un mese.

6. Marco è italiano, _____   f. a casa tardi.

7. Sono a Venezia _____   g. ma vive a New York.

8. Questa camicia è _____   h. di Carla fa la cantante.

9. La madre _____   i. da Roma?

10. Viterbo è lontano _____   j. di cotone.

Complete the sentences with the appropriate prepositions.

1. Mia sorella abita _____ via Mantova 16, _____ un palazzo elegante.

2. Quando sono _____ Italia, preferisco viaggiare _____ treno.

3. Quell'attrice è _____ Glasgow, ma vive _____ New York _____ il marito e il figlio.

4. Mamma, c'è qualcosa _____ mangiare e _____ bere _____ casa?

5. Perché vuoi andare _____ America? _____ lavoro?

6. Tuo nonno ha cominciato _____ lavorare _____ dodici anni!

7. Quest'estate vado _____ Capri e _____ Sardegna, e poi parto _____ il Brasile.

8. Mio marito insegna _____ settembre _____ giugno.

9. L'aereo parte _____ mezzora!

10. Ho telefonato _____ Marco un'ora fa.

Prepositions in other roles

Some prepositions can also function as adverbs, adjectives, and verbs. The following words are prepositions only when they are followed by a noun, an adjective, or another preposition. As prepositions, they are invariable.

attraverso	*through*
durante	*during*
entro	*by (a certain amount of time)*
salvo, tranne	*except*
meno	*less*
secondo	*according*
lungo	*along*
malgrado	*despite*

Since some of the preceding prepositions also double as adjectives, it is important to identify what is being described in order to use them correctly.

Cammino **lungo** (prep.) la strada.   Il Pò è il fiume più **lungo** (adj.) d'Italia.
I walk along the road.   *The Pò is the longest river in Italy.*

The following prepositions are generally followed by a noun, either explicitly or implied:

contro il muro   **dentro** casa   **dietro** il ristorante
against the wall   *inside the house*   *behind the restaurant*

senza sale   **verso** sera
without salt   *towards evening*

When these prepositions are followed by a personal pronoun, **di** is added before the pronoun.

contro di me   **dentro** di noi   **dietro** di te   **senza** di me   **verso** di lui
against me   *inside us*   *behind you*   *without me*   *toward him*

Other prepositions require **a**, **da**, or **di** when followed by a noun or pronoun. I recommend learning these as phrases rather than as separate words.

accanto a	*next to*
davanti a	*in front of*
rispetto a	*regarding*
grazie a	*thanks to*
insieme a / con	*together with*
fino a	*until*
vicino a	*near to*
lontano da	*far from*
prima di	*before*
invece di	*instead of*

Some prepositional phrases consist of two prepositions. These too are better learned as phrases.

in mezzo a	*in the midst of*
in base a	*based on*
in cima a	*at the top of*
in seguito a	*following*
al di là di	*beyond*
a causa di	*because of*
a destra / sinistra di	*to the right / left of*
a eccezione di	*except for*

Combined prepositions (**le preposizioni articolate**)

When the prepositions **di, in, a, da**, and **su** are followed by a definite article, they combine with the article and form a single word, as shown in this table:

	il	lo	l'	la	i	gli	le
a	al	allo	all'	alla	ai	agli	alle
di	del	dello	dell'	della	dei	degli	delle
da	dal	dallo	dall'	dalla	dai	dagli	dalle
in	nel	nello	nell'	nella	nei	negli	nelle
su	sul	sullo	sull'	sulla	sui	sugli	sulle
con	col				coi		

Nota bene

1. The prepositions **a, da**, and **su** do not change their spelling when they combine.
2. The prepositions **di** and **in** change to **de** and **ne** before combining with the definite article.
3. All the other articles simply combine with the proposition, and whenever the article begins with -**l**, it is doubled.
4. The preposition **con** may combine with the article by dropping the -**n**; however, this form is slowly disappearing in spoken Italian. It appears mainly in opera librettos or literary works.

Prepositions and idiomatic expressions

Prepositional phrases are often used idiomatically and seem to be more difficult to translate into English than other words. They cannot always be translated literally into English. These phrases are said to be "crystalized," or fixed, since they cannot be changed. They are typical of native and informal speech and you should try to use them whenever possible. Here is a list to get you started. A close Italian equivalent is given in the second column.

IDIOMATIC EXPRESSION	EQUIVALENT EXPRESSION	ENGLISH TRANSLATION
di buon'ora	presto	*early*
di gran lunga	moltissimo	*by far*
di punto in bianco	all'improvviso	*suddenly*
a bruciapelo	velocemente	*point-blank*
andare a finire	concludersi	*to end up*
a lungo andare	dopo molto tempo	*in the long run*
a mala pena	con difficoltà	*barely*
a quattr'occhi	privatamente	*in private*
alla buona	semplicemente	*simply*
in gamba	con molte qualità	*to have your act together*
con le mani in mano	senza fare niente	*idle, not lifting a finger*
su due piedi	immediatamente	*at once, quickly*
su per giù	all'incirca	*more or less*
sulle spine	nervoso, preoccupato	*worried*
darsi da fare	prendere iniziativa	*to get busy*
faccio per dire	voglio dire	*I mean*
stare per	accingersi a	*to be about to*

Combine the prepositions with the articles.

1. L'albergo è vicino (a + la) _____ chiesa.

2. Non mettere i gomiti (*elbows*) (su + il) _____ tavolo!

3. Quel negozio apre (a + le) _____ 9.00.

4. E chiuso (da + le) _____ 14.00 (a + le) _____ 16.00.

5. La pensione è aperta (da + il) _____ mese di giugno.

6. Dante nacque (in + il) _____ 1265.

7. Non camminare (su + i) _____ fiori!

8. Gli animali non stanno bene (a + lo) _____ zoo.

Fill in the blanks with the correct simple or combined prepositions, as needed.

1. Vado _____ casa presto perché sono stanca.

2. Ci vediamo _____ stazione?

3. C'è un bel film _____ cinema Rialto _____ mezzanotte.

4. Vado _____ lavoro in autobus, ma quando fa bello vado _____ piedi.

5. Se vuoi spendere di meno è meglio andare _____ pizzeria.

6. Ci sono moltissime fontane _____ Roma.

7. Vuoi venire _____ Sicilia con noi? Possiamo andare tutti _____ mia zia.

8. Voglio stare _____ spiaggia _____ mattina _____ sera!

Problematic prepositions

It is an unfortunate truth that the smaller words such as articles and prepositions tend to cause the most problems for learners of Italian. Memorizing common prepositions in the context of short phrases will help them "stick," and as you notice new phrases you can make a list so that they will come to mind more easily as you speak.

a casa	*at home*
a teatro	*to the theater*
a piedi	*on foot*
a scuola	*to school*
a letto	*to bed*
in Italia	*to Italy*
in treno	*by train*
in cucina	*in the kitchen*
in realtà	*actually*

in effetti	*actually*
in ogni caso	*in any case*
tra noi/fra noi	*between us*
da Giovanni	*to Giovanni's place, home*
da piccolo/a	*as a child*
scarpe da tennis	*tennis shoes*
molto da fare	*a lot to do*
qualcosa da bere	*something to drink*
di Roberto	*Roberto's*
di mattina	*in the morning*
di sera	*in the evening*
di solito	*usually*
di niente	*don't mention it*

ESERCIZIO
15·5

Review the preceding list, and then translate the following common phrases from English to Italian on your own. Check the answer key; mark the ones you missed and review them again.

1. *I am going by bike.*

_____

2. *I usually eat early.*

_____

3. *I live in Rome.*

_____

4. *Let's go to Silvio's place.*

_____

5. *I am going on foot.*

_____

6. *It's 8:00 in the morning.*

_____

7. *I have a lot to do.*

_____

8. *I actually prefer sparkling water.*

_____

9. *Don't mention it!*

_____

10. *He was very blonde as a child.*

_____

The following sentences contain a number of incorrect prepositions (number noted in parentheses). Find the errors and correct them. Check the answer key for accuracy. For extra practice, translate them into English and then back into Italian. Compare your translations with the answer key and indicate the errors.

1. Abito in Roma, e vado a lavoro nella metropolitana (*subway*). (2)

   _____

   _____

2. Studia quasi sempre nel salotto. (1)

   _____

   _____

3. Sei tornata alla casa tardi? (1)

   _____

   _____

4. Stasera andiamo al teatro. (1)

   _____

   _____

5. Parto a Roma nell'aereo. (2)

   _____

   _____

6. Vado in casa della mia sorella. (2) (**Nota:** Sentence can be reduced to four words.)

   _____

   _____

7. Perché hai messo le scarpe per tennis? (1)

   _____

   _____

8. Domani pomeriggio ho un appuntamento al dentista. (1)

   _____

   _____

9. Gli italiani non vanno sempre nella chiesa. (1)

   _____

   _____

10. Vuoi qualcosa per mangiare? (1)

_____

_____

ESERCIZIO

15·7

Read aloud the following sentences several times. Prepositions and idioms that often cause errors are in boldface. You can expand this exercise by repeating the sentences in the negative and changing the tenses and subjects, until the highlighted elements become automatic.

1. **Fanno** colazione a casa.   *They have breakfast at home.*

2. **Faccio** un bagno caldo.   *I take a hot bath.*

3. Perché **fai** sempre tardi?   *Why are you always late?*

4. **Escono di** casa presto.   *They leave the house early.*

5. **Prendo** un caffè la mattina.   *I have a coffee in the morning.*

6. Ho **un sacco da** fare.   *I have a lot of stuff to do.*

7. **Finisce di** lavorare tardi.   *She finishes work late.*

8. **Andiamo in** palestra?   *Shall we go to the gym?*

9. Come **va**?   *How is it going?*

10. Mi vesto **in fretta**.   *I get dressed in a hurry.*

ESERCIZIO

15·8

Translate the following words and phrases, but be careful!

1. *something to drink*

_____

2. *usually*

_____

3. *by train*

_____

4. *in Venice*

_____

5. *a lot to do*

_____

6. *actually*

_____

7. *between us*

_____

8. *in any case*

_____

9. *on foot*

_____

10. *at my place*

_____

Pronouns

There are many types of pronouns, and their main function is to replace nouns (*pronoun* means "in place of" or "for the noun") to avoid repetition and to simplify the discourse. In this section, we will discuss subject and object pronouns in their unstressed forms, which generally precede the verb, as well as the emphatic forms, which generally follow the verb or preposition.

Subject pronouns

In English the subject pronoun is almost always expressed, since most regular verbs do not conjugate at all, except for the third-person singular.

In Italian, however, the subject pronoun is generally omitted, since the subject is also expressed through the verb ending. Having both the subject pronoun and the verb ending, therefore, is redundant and is simplified by dropping the pronoun.

io	*I*	noi	*we*
tu	*you*	voi	*you (plural)*
lui/lei, Lei (*formal*)	*she, he, it, you (formal)*	loro, Loro	*they, you (formal)*

There are, however, some cases when the subject pronoun is used:

1. when the pronoun is being emphasized or to avoid ambiguity or confusion. In English speech, this is done by emphasizing the pronoun with the voice, and in writing, it is underlined or put it in italics.

2. after the word **anche**, which means *also*

    Anch'**io** vengo al cinema!

3. in questions—the pronoun is sometimes added at the end of the sentence

4. to replace a whole verb phrase

    Vengo anch'*io*!   No, tu no!
    I'm coming, too!   *No, you're not!*

    Sto bene, e **tu**?
    I'm well, and you?

If you leave out the subject pronouns in the following Italian sentences, the meaning and emphasis change slightly. Emphasis is frequently used in irony and humor, and learning when to use the pronouns will make your Italian more native and idiomatic. When the pronouns are used, they can be emphasized further as follows:

- by putting them after the verb, as in example 2, or at the end of a question, as in example 3

1. **Io** cucino, mentre **lui** si rilassa.	*I cook, while **he** takes it easy.*
2. Sono stati **loro** a farlo.	*They're the ones who did it.*
3. Francesco, sei proprio **tu**?	*Francesco, is it really **you**?*

- after **come** or **quanto** (**io** and **tu** are replaced by **me** and **te**)

Ho studiato quanto **lui**.	Siamo partiti presto come **voi**.
*I studied as much as **he**.*	*We left as early as **you**.*

- after the words **anche** (**pure**), **neanche** (**neppure**), **nemmeno**, and **proprio**

Anch'**io** parto con quel volo.	Neanche **lui** vuole andare alla festa.
I'm also leaving on the same flight.	*He doesn't want to go to the party either.*

- in exclamations and phrases without a verb (**io** and **tu** are replaced by **me** and **te**)

Beato **lui**! Povera **te**!	Chi ha vinto? **Lui**.
Lucky him! Poor me!	*Who won? He did.*

When using the formal **Lei** or **Loro** in writing, it is generally capitalized for clarity. The plural formal **Loro** is gradually disappearing and being replaced by **voi**.

ESERCIZIO
16·1

Add the correct subject pronoun in the following sentences.

1. Anche _____ vogliono fare un viaggio in Messico.

2. Neanch' _____ uso macchina. Preferisco andare a piedi o in bicicletta.

3. Questa volta offro _____!

4. Vieni alla festa anche _____?

5. Perché non vanno anche _____ in Italia?

6. Come state _____ e tuo marito?

7. È vero che _____ è una scrittrice molto famosa?

8. Come si chiama _____? Si chiama Marcello.

9. Scusi, ma _____ come si chiama? (*formal*)

Direct-object pronouns

A direct object is a noun that is directly affected by the action of the verb. It usually follows the verb directly, without a preposition, and identifies the thing or person being acted upon. It answers the question *What . . . ?* or *Whom . . . ?* (in colloquial English *Who . . . ?*)

> *What are you reading? I am reading an **article** by my professor.*
> *Whom (who) are you inviting? I am inviting **Giorgia**.*

The nouns that immediately follow the verbs in the above examples are direct objects of the verb. When referring back to these nouns, instead of repeating them again and again, one can replace them with direct-object pronouns. This avoids useless repetition of the nouns and greatly simplifies communication. Look at the following conversation and notice how the noun **articolo** *(article)* is referred to in the second sentence.

Cosa leggi?
What are you reading?

Leggo un **articolo** del mio professore. (**Articolo** is the direct object.)
*I'm reading an **article** by my professor.*

Anch'io **lo** voglio leggere. (The pronoun **lo** replaces the noun **articolo**.)
*I want to read **it**, too.*

Chi inviti a cena?
Who/whom are you inviting to dinner?

Invito **Giorgia**. (**Giorgia** is the direct object.)
*I'm inviting **Giorgia**.*

La inviti anche al cinema? (The direct-object pronoun **la** replaces the direct object, **Giorgia**.)
*Are you inviting **her** to the movies, too?*

For many learners replacing the object with a pronoun can be challenging. In English, *it* replaces all inanimate things, and speakers do not have to think of these nouns as feminine or masculine. Another problem is how the word order changes when object pronouns are introduced. In English, the direct-object pronoun always comes after the verb. As you can see in the Italian examples above, the object pronoun goes before the verb. Practice and repetition will eventually lead to a smooth and automatic use of these pronouns.

A good way to learn the direct-object pronouns is to observe them carefully and to look for patterns. First of all, you may notice that they are two letters long, and that the first- and second-person pronouns, **mi**, **ti**, **ci**, and **vi** all end with the letter **-i** and are identical to the reflexive pronouns. You may also notice that only the third-person pronouns reflect gender and number, with the same final vowels used in nouns and adjectives, **-o**, **-a**, **-i**, and **-e**. By noticing these patterns and finding others on your own, you will find that they will be securely anchored in your memory and will be there when you need to use them.

mi	*me*
ti	*you*
lo/la	*it, her/him*
ci	*us*
vi	*you*
li/le	*them*

When used with an infinitive verb, the pronoun attaches to the end of the verb, which drops the final **-e**.

È importante studiare i pronomi.   È importante studiar**li**.   *It is important to study them.*

But with the modal verbs **dovere**, **volere**, and **potere** + infinitive, the pronoun can either precede the conjugated modal or attach to the infinitive.

Voglio salutar**lo**.   *or*   **Lo** voglio salutare.   *I want to greet him.*

Only the singular pronouns **lo** and **la** may elide with a word that starts with a vowel or a silent **h**.

Romeo **l'**ama.   **L'**hanno visto a Verona.
Romeo loves her.   *They saw him in Verona.*

Extra challenge

When used with a compound tense, the participle must agree with the third-person direct-object pronouns **lo**, **la**, **li**, **le**, and **ne** in gender and number. The agreement with the other persons is optional and is gradually disappearing. Agreement does not occur with indirect-object pronouns.

Dove hai comprato quelle **scarpe**?
Where did you buy those shoes?

Le ho comprat**e** a Milano.
I bought them in Milan.

Hai invitato Liliana?
Did you invite Liliana?

Sì, l'ho invitat**a**, ma non **le ho detto** che veniva il suo ex.
Yes, I invited her, but didn't tell her that her ex-boyfriend was coming.

ESERCIZIO
16·2

*Answer the questions using a direct-object pronoun. For an extra challenge, recast the question in the **passato prossimo**, remembering the agreement with the participle in the response.*

ESEMPIO   Compri la pasta?
Sì, _la_ compro.
Hai comprato la pasta?
Sì, l'ho comprata.

1. Vedi le tue amiche questo weekend? Sì, _____ vedo.

_____? _____

2. Studi la matematica? No, non _____ studio.

_____? _____

3. Guardi la TV? No, non _____ guardo.

_____? _____

4. Parli il cinese in classe? Sì, _____ parlo.

_____? _____

5. Leggi i giornali italiani? Sì, _____ leggo.

_____? _____

Indirect-object pronouns

In some sentences the noun object indicates not what but *to whom* or *for whom* the action is being carried out. In Italian the indirect-object nouns are preceded by the prepositions **a** or **per**, which indicate the object as indirect. As recipients, indirect objects are usually people or living things. The pronouns that replace them are identical to the direct-object pronouns, except for the third-person forms as shown below. Like the other pronouns, they precede the conjugated verb and attach to the infinitive verb. When used with the modal verbs **dovere**, **potere**, and **volere**, the pronouns can either go before the conjugated verb or attach to the infinitive.

to me	mi	*to us*	ci
to you	ti	*to you all*	vi
to him	gli (*m.*)	*to them*	gli (*m. + f.*) (*loro)
to her	le (*f.*)		

*In contemporary speech, the third-person plural form **loro** has been replaced by **gli**.

How important is it to be able to distinguish a direct object from an indirect object? Since both types of pronouns share the same forms in the first and second person, unless you are using the third-person pronouns, it may not seem to matter. Noticing that certain verbs commonly use a preposition before the object, and memorizing verb + preposition as one (**parlare con, comprare per**, etc.), will lead to a deeper understanding of Italian sentence structure, will improve comprehension, and, most importantly, will give you more confidence.

The following is a list of verbs that take direct objects, indirect objects, or both.

DIRECT		INDIRECT		DIRECT AND INDIRECT	
amare	*to love*	mancare a	*to be missing*	chiedere	*to ask*
ascoltare	*to listen*	parere a	*to seem to*	dare	*to give*
bere	*to drink*	piacere a	*to be pleasing to*	dire	*to say*
chiamare	*to call*	rispondere a	*to answer*	fare	*to do*
conoscere	*to know*	sembrare a	*to seem to*	leggere	*to read*
guardare	*to look at*			mandare	*to send*
invitare	*to invite*			offrire	*to offer*
mangiare	*to eat*			portare	*to bring*
perdere	*to lose*			regalare	*to give a gift*
prendere	*to take*			scrivere	*to write*
sentire	*to hear*			vendere	*to sell*
studiare	*to study*				
trovare	*to find*				
vedere	*to see*				

Nota bene

There are some verbs that take a direct object in English but an indirect object in Italian.

INDIRECT	DIRECT
chiedere a	*to ask*
dire a	*to tell*
rispondere a	*to answer*
telefonare a	*to phone*
piacere a	*to please*

There are also those that take a direct object in Italian but an indirect object in English.

DIRECT	INDIRECT
ascoltare	*to listen to*
aspettare	*to wait for*

Identify the object in each sentence as direct or indirect and rewrite the questions using the appropriate pronoun.

1. Bevi l'acqua minerale?

_____

2. Parli spesso con Susanna?

_____

3. Telefoni alla tua amica?

_____

4. Mangi gli spaghetti?

_____

5. Ai tuoi genitori piace il tuo ragazzo?

_____

6. Conosci quel cantante bravissimo?

_____

7. Vuoi scrivere ad Annamaria e Letizia?

_____

8. Cosa dici alla tua amica?

_____

Stressed pronouns (i pronomi tonici)

Stressed pronouns are used after a preposition, and unlike the direct- and indirect-object pronouns, they follow the verb. Except for the first- and second-person singular, they are the same as the subject pronouns.

me	noi
te	voi
lui/lei	loro

The reflexive stressed pronouns are the same as the preceding except for the third-person singular and plural, which is **sé**. When stressing the reflexive pronoun, it is common to follow the reflexive pronoun with **stesso** or to use the preposition **da** before the pronoun.

Conosci **te stesso**.	*Know yourself.*
Mio figlio di tre anni si lava **da sé**.	*My three-year-old son washes himself on his own.*

When **da** is used to indicate someone's home, office, or place it is always followed by either a proper name or a stressed pronoun.

Andiamo da lei!	*We're going to her place.*
Venite da me per un caffè.	*Come to my place for a coffee.*

Stressed pronouns can be used for emphasis, but one should be careful not to overuse them. The unstressed forms occur much more frequently in native speech, and although stressed pronouns happen to follow the same word order as English, they do not have the same meaning. Here are some sentences that illustrate the difference:

Ti chiamo domani. (unstressed pronoun)
I'll call you tomorrow.

Chiamo **te** domani. (stressed pronoun)
I'll call __you__ tomorrow. (as opposed to someone else)

Mi dica, signora Rossi. (unstressed pronoun)
Tell me, Mrs. Rossi.

Dica **a me,** signora Rossi. (stressed pronoun)
Tell __me__, Mrs. Rossi. (as opposed to someone else)

Nota bene

When emphasizing a pronoun, one must be careful to use the correct type of pronoun, which may be an object, subject, or reflexive pronoun. The subject pronoun often follows the verb when emphasized.

Sono io.   *It's me (I).*
Paghi tu?   *Are __you__ paying?*

ESERCIZIO
16·4

Translate the following sentences using stressed object or subject pronouns.

1. *I speak with __him__ every day.*

   _____

2. *__You__ always pay!*

   _____

3. *Come (sing.) to my place!*

   _____

4. *I'm going out with them tonight.*

   _____

5. *Do you need me tomorrow?*

   _____

6. *Can I count on you (plural)?*

   _____

7. *He always talks about himself!*

   _____

8. *There's a message for you.*

_____

9. *I fell in love with him.* (**innamorarsi**)

_____

10. *According to him they are arriving tomorrow.*

_____

Prepositions + di + pronouns

The following prepositions add **di** before a pronoun. The same prepositions, when followed by a noun, omit **di**. In English, these prepositions stand alone, whether they are followed by a pronoun or a noun. It is important to make this distinction when using the following prepositions.

contro *against*	Hai qualcosa **contro di me**? *Do you have something against me?*	Metti lo scaffale **contro il muro**. *Put the bookshelf against the wall.*
dietro *behind*	C'è un uomo strano **dietro di noi**. *There is a strange man behind us.*	**Dietro la porta** c'è la scopa. *Behind the door there is a broom.*
dopo *after*	**Dopo di me** c'è la signora. *The lady is after me.*	Arriverò **dopo le due**. *I will arrive after 2.*
fra / tra *in / between*	C'è tensione **fra di loro**. *There's tension between them.*	La lampada è **fra i due letti**. *The lamp is between the two beds.*
senza *without*	Non posso vivere **senza di te**! *I can't live without you!*	Mangi la pasta **senza il parmigiano**? *Do you eat pasta without parmigiano?*
sopra *above*	**Sopra di noi** ci sono degli studenti. *Above us there are some students.*	Lo specchio è **sopra il lavandino**. *The mirror is above the sink.*
sotto *underneath*	**Sotto di noi** non c'è nessuno. *Underneath us there is no one.*	Il cane va sempre **sotto il letto**. *The dog always sleeps under the bed.*
su *on*	Puoi contare **su di me**! *You can count on me!*	Il giornale è **sul tavolo**. *The newspaper is on the table.*

Non voglio parlare **di lui** stasera.	*I don't want to talk **about him** tonight.*
Ho comprato un regalo **per loro**.	*I bought a gift for <u>them</u>.*

ci

Ci is used most frequently as a direct, indirect, or reflexive pronoun.

Volete venire a cena?	*Do you want to come to dinner?*
Che cosa **ci** prepari?	*What will you make for us?*
Arriveder**ci**!	*Until we see each other again.*
Io e mio fratello **ci** svegliamo (reflexive) sempre tardi.	*My brother and I always get up late.*

Ci is frequently used to express the general idea of existence or being in the verb **esserci**.

Pronto, **c'è** Paola?	*Hello, **is** Paola **there**?*
C'è qualche problema?	***Is there** some problem?*

Before the vowels **e** or **i**, **ci** is usually elided. In writing it is never elided to a letter that will change its pronunciation, but in speaking it is often pronounced without the **i** sound.

C'erano molte persone al concerto.	***There were** a lot of people at the concert.*
Mi dispiace, non **ci ho** pensato.	*I'm sorry, I didn't think **about it**.*

Ci can be used to replace a prepositional phrase introduced by **a, in, su,** or **da** followed by a place or location. In this case, **ci** functions as an adverb of place, meaning *there*. It either precedes the conjugated verb or follows the infinitive or gerund.

Siete andati **all'opera**?	*Did you go to the opera?*
Sì, **ci** siamo stati ieri sera.	*Yes, we went (there) last night.*
Vai spesso in palestra?	*Do you often go to the gym?*
Cerco di **andarci** almeno tre volte a settimana.	*I try to go (there) at least three times a week.*

Ci can be used to replace **a, di,** or **con** followed by a noun.

Ripensando **alla mia carriera**, forse avrei dovuto studiare ingegneria.
Thinking back on my career, maybe I should have studied engineering.

Ripensando**ci**, forse avrei dovuto studiare ingegneria.
*Thinking back **on it**, maybe I should have studied engineering.*

Non capisco **l'economia**.	*I don't understand economics.*
Anch'io non **ci capisco** niente.	*I don't understand anything (about it) either.*

Ho visto la mia professoressa di italiano e **ci** ho parlato a lungo.
*I saw my Italian professor and talked **with her** a long time.*

Ci can be used to replace **a** followed by an infinitive phrase.

Riesci **a vedere** la strada?	*Can you see the road?*
Non **ci** riesco, c'è troppa nebbia.	*No, I can't see it, there's too much fog.*

Some verbs used with the particle **ci** take on an alternate meaning:

◆ **entrarci** (*to have to do with*)

Mia sorella **non c'entra** niente!	*My sister has **nothing to do with** this!*

◆ **metterci** (*to take time*)

Quanto **ci metti** a scrivere questa tesi?	*How long **is it taking you** to write this thesis?*

◆ **volerci** (*to take [time, money. etc.]*)

Quante **ore ci vogliono**?	**Ci vuole** una mezza giornata.
How many hours does it take?	*It takes a half a day.*

With **volerci** the amount becomes the subject. It takes **essere** as an auxiliary, and therefore, the participle agrees with the subject (the amount of time, money, etc.):

Per andare da Roma a Chicago **ci sono volute** otto ore.
To go from Rome to Chicago it took us eight hours.

Quanto **ci vuole** per comprare un appartamento a Venezia?
How much do you need to buy an apartment in Venice?

Ci vogliono almeno duecentomila euro.
At least 200,000 euros (are needed.)

ne

Ne is another small word that is very useful. It is important to know that **ne** is not a negative! Like **ci**, it is invariable and is used as a partitive pronoun to express quantity or number. In English, a number can be used alone to express quantity, but in Italian expressions of quantity are generally followed by a noun. These phrases of quantity can be replaced by the object pronoun **ne**, which means *of it/them*.

Quante rosette desidera?	*How many rolls do you want?*
Ne vorrei tre, per favore.	*I would like three (of them), please.*
Quanti pomodori vuole?	*How many tomatoes do you want?*
Ne prendo un chilo.	*I'll take two pounds (of them).*

In the responses, **ne** replaces the object modified by an expression of quantity.
  Ne can also be used with an indefinite quantity.

Hai amici italiani?	*Do you have Italian friends?*
Ne ho moltissimi.	*I have a lot of them.*

Ne can replace a prepositional phrase introduced by **di** or **da**.

Parli **di politica** con i tuoi genitori?	*Do you talk about politics with your parents?*
Non, non **ne** parlo.	*No, I don't talk (about it).*
Hai bisogno **di** questo libro?	*Do you need this book?*
No, grazie. Non **ne** ho bisogno.	*No, thanks. I don't have a need (of it).*
Appena l'ho visto, **ne** sono rimasta innamorata. (di lui)	*As soon as I saw him, I fell in love (with him).*
Quando è uscito **dall'aula**?	*When did he come out of the classroom?*
Ne è uscito poco fa. (dall'aula)	*He came out (of it) a little while ago.*

With transitive verbs in a compound tense, **ne** is treated like a direct-object pronoun, and the participle agrees in gender and in number with the noun being replaced.

Quanti **libri** hai comprato?	*How many books did you buy?*
Ne ho comprat**i** tre.	*I bought three (of them).*

ESERCIZIO
16·5

*Answer the following questions using **ci** or **ne**.*

1. Quando vai a Roma? _____ vado in giugno.

2. Quanto anni ha tuo fratello? _____ ha 23.

3. Parli mai della tua adolescenza? Non _____ parlo quasi mai.

4. Quando arriviamo a Pisa? _____ vorranno almeno due ore.

5. Hai più sentito Luigi? Non _____ parlo da almeno tre anni.

6. Prenderai una BMW? Non _____ penso nemmeno, costa troppo.

7. Quando è uscito dal cinema? _____ è uscito poco fa.

8. Hai paura dei ragni? _____ ho una paura estrema!

9. Quando torni a Como? _____ tornerò l'estate prossima.

10. Credi nella telepatia? Sì, _____ credo.

Double-object pronouns

Leggi **le favole** <u>al tuo fratellino</u>?   *Do you read **fairy tales** <u>to your little brother</u>?*

In the preceding sentence there is a direct object (*fairy tales*) followed by the recipient, or indirect object (*your little brother*).

Many verbs can be followed by both a direct and indirect object. The indirect object can be singular or plural (**mi, ti, gli, le, ci, vi, gli**) while the direct object will always be third-person singular or plural (**lo, la, li, le**). Both objects can be replaced by double-object pronouns, which combine the indirect and the direct-object pronouns into one word or phrase, as we will see later, and place them before the conjugated verb or attached to the infinitive verb.

The first- and second-person indirect-object pronouns (**mi, ti, ci, vi**) always precede the direct-object pronouns, and when combined change to **me, te, ce,** and **ve**. The direct-object pronouns **lo, la, li, le,** and **ne** will follow as a separate word unless the infinitive is being used, in which case, they are combined and attached to the end of the infinitive. To help you distinguish them, the direct objects are in bold and the indirect objects are underlined.

<u>Mi</u> passi **il sale**?   <u>Me</u> **lo** passi?
*Can you pass **the salt** <u>to me</u>?*   *Can you pass **it** <u>to me</u>?*

<u>Ti</u> mando **una mail**.   <u>Te</u> **la** mando oggi.
*I'll send <u>you</u> **an e-mail**.*   *I'll send **it** <u>to you</u> today.*

<u>Ci</u> date **i vostri indirizzi**?   <u>Ce</u> **li** date?
*Can you give <u>us</u> **your addresses**?*   *Can you give **them** <u>to us</u>?*

Dove possiamo mandar<u>vi</u> **dei fiori**?   Dove possiamo mandar<u>ve</u>**li**?
*Where can we send <u>you</u> **some flowers**?*   *Where can we send **them** <u>to you</u>?*

When the third-person indirect-object pronouns **le** and **gli** combine with the direct-object pronouns, they both change to **glie-**, to which **lo, la, li, le,** or **ne** attach and form one word.

Gli or **le** + **lo, la, li, le** → glielo, gliela, glieli, gliele

This is the form of all four possible indirect-object pronouns in the third person (*to her, to him, to you* [formal], and *to them*).

Hai dato **la foto** <u>a Sofia</u>?   Sì, <u>glie</u>**lo**'ho data.
*Did you give **the photo** <u>to Sofia</u>?*   *Yes, I gave **it** <u>to her</u>.*

Mandiamo **una cartolina**   *Shall we send a **postcard** to*
    <u>a Marina e Roberto</u>?   <u>Marina and Roberto</u>?
Sì, <u>glie</u>**la** mandiamo da Roma.   *Yes, we'll send it from Rome.*

Agreement of third-person direct-object pronouns in compound tenses

When using object pronouns in compound tenses such as **passato prossimo**, **condizionale passato**, etc., the participle must agree with the direct-object pronouns **lo**, **la**, **li**, **le**, and **ne** in gender and number.

Ti ho mandato **le ricette**?
*Did I send you **the recipes**?*

Ti hanno dato **la promozione**?
*Did they give you **the promotion**?*

Te le ho mandate?
*Did I send **them to you**?*

Te l'hanno data?
*Did they give **it to you**?*

ESERCIZIO
16·6

Simplify the sentences using double-object pronouns, as in the example. If it helps you, indicate the indirect object in the sentence. Remember the agreement between the direct-object pronouns and the participle.

ESEMPIO   Hai preparato <u>la pasta</u> per gli amici ? *Glie l'hai preparata?*

1. Hai comprato i libri per la tua amica? _____

2. Hai riportato il libro al professore? _____

3. Dai il giornale alla nonna, per favore? _____

4. Hai prestato la macchina ai tuoi amici? _____

5. Consiglieresti l'ultimo film di Woody Allen ai tuoi genitori? _____

6. Puoi prendermi una bottiglia di acqua minerale? _____

7. Tuo padre ti regala una Fiat 500 per il tua compleanno? _____

8. Marina vi ha dato i biglietti per l'opera? _____

9. Hai regalato tre DVD a tuo cugino? (Use ne) _____

10. Hai insegnato quell'aria di Mozart alla tua studentessa? _____

Numbers

Cardinal numbers are used to count and to express quantity and are generally invariable. From 0–999 only the number *one* (**uno**) changes when followed by a noun and may function as an indefinite article. **Mille** (*one thousand*) changes to **mila** in the plural, and **milione** (*million*) and **miliardo** (*trillion*) have plural forms (**milioni** and **miliardi**).

Ordinal numbers are used to indicate order or rank. They are adjectives and therefore agree with the noun they are modifying. The ordinal numbers after tenth (**decimo**) are formed by dropping the last vowel of the cardinal number and adding **-esimo/a**. Ordinal numbers are also written as Roman numerals when indicating centuries or the order of succession of monarchs, emperors, popes, etc.

Il XV secolo	*the fifteenth century*
Enrico VIII	*Henry the eighth*

	ROMAN	CARDINAL	ORDINAL	
0		zero		
1	I	uno	primo	1º, 1ª
2	II	due	secondo	2º, 2ª
3	III	tre	terzo	
4	IV	quattro	quarto	
5	V	cinque	quinto	
6	VI	sei	sesto	
7	VII	sette	settimo	
8	VIII	otto	ottavo	
9	IX	nove	nono	
10	X	dieci	decimo	
11	XI	undici	undicesimo	
12	XII	dodici	dodicesimo	
13	XIII	tredici	tredicesimo	
14	XIV	quattordici	quattordicesimo	
15	XV	quindici	quindicesimo	
16	XVI	sedici	sedicesimo	
17	XVII	diciassette	diciassettesimo	
18	XVIII	diciotto	diciottesimo	
19	XIX	diciannove	diciannovesimo	
20	XX	venti	ventesimo	
21	XXI	ventuno	ventunesimo	
26	XXVI	ventisei	ventiseiesimo	
28	XXVIII	ventotto	ventottesimo	
29	XXIX	ventinove	ventinovesimo	
33	XXXIII	trentatré	trentatreesimo	

Attenzione!

Sei drops the **-i** in **sedici** and **sessanta** but keeps it in the ordinal numbers.

  ventiseiesimo   centoseiesimo

Nota bene

The number **tre** needs an accent when it forms the last syllable of a cardinal number.

  trentatré   quarantatré

Ordinal numbers are also used to express fractions.

  un terzo   1/3   due terzi   2/3
  un quarto   1/4   tre quarti   3/4

Attenzione!

When the number **uno**, or any number that ends with **uno** (**ventuno, trentuno, centouno**), is followed by a noun, it follows the same rules as the singular indefinite article. As a result, the gender of the noun that follows it will determine its form.

  Ci sono **trentuno** studenti nella classe. (followed by **s** + consonant)
  There are thirty-one students in the class.

  Agosto ha **trentun giorni**. (followed by a consonant other than **z**, **s** + consonant, etc.)
  August has thirty-one days.

  Mio figlio ha **ventun anni**. (when followed by a vowel, as with the indefinite article, it is
    written without an apostrophe)
  My son is twenty-one.

Numbers ending in **tre**, such as **ventitré**, must be written with an accent to keep the stress on the final syllable.

Numbers are usually written out as numerals, but when they are written out as words, such as when writing a check, numbers under a million are generally written as one word.

  trecentoquarantatré   milleottocento   duemiladodici
  three hundred forty three   *one thousand eight hundred*   *two thousand twelve*

Dates are read the same as cardinal numbers and do not divide into hundreds as in English.

  1482   millequattrocentonovantadue   2003   duemilatré

When referring to a whole century, one can use:

  il '700   il settecento (which means the 1700s)

or use a Roman numeral:

  il XVII secolo (read as **il diciassettesimo secolo**)

Numbers that begin with **milione** or **miliardo** are written separately and have a plural form:

  due milioni trecentomila   un miliardo duecentonovantamilaottantacinque

When **milione** and **miliardo** are followed by another noun, the preposition **di** must be used:

  un milione **di** persone   tre miliardi **di** dollari
  a million people   *three billion dollars*

Nota bene

Multiples of a thousand are separated by a period, while decimals are indicated by a comma (**virgola**) and are read as follows:

1.298.360	un milione duecentonovantottomilatrecentosessanta
98,06	novantotto virgola zerosei

Phone numbers

The Italian area code, or **prefisso**, generally begins with a zero (two digits for big cities, three digits for medium cities, and four digits for small towns) and is followed by the phone number, which is read in groups of 2-2-3.

The following number 0521 2637902 is read:

zero cinque due uno – due sei–tre sette–nove zero due

or

ventisei – trentasette–novecentodue

Numerical expressions

Here are some numerical expressions and terms used in everyday speech:

un paio	*a pair*
una coppia	*a pair* or *a couple*
una dozzina	*a dozen*
una ventina, una trentina, etc.	*circa twenty, around thirty*, etc.
un centinaio	*circa one hundred*
un migliaio	*circa one thousand*
pari	*even*
dispari	*odd*

Attenzione!

The words **pari** (*even*) and **dispari** (*odd*) are invariable adjectives, so their endings never change to show agreement.

un numero pari	*an even number*	un numero <u>dispari</u>	*an odd number*

There are prefixes that indicate number of months, years, and musical groupings.

trimestre	**se**mestre		
decennio	**vent**ennio		
duetto	**terz**etto	**du**o	**tri**o

Telling time

To ask the time in Italian, we ask:

Che **ora** è?	*What hour is it?* or
Che **ore** sono?	*What hours are they?*

The noun **ora** is feminine and is preceded by the definite article as follows:

E` l'una.

One o'clock is the only feminine singular hour and uses the third-person singular verb.

The remaining hours are plural and use the third-person plural form of **essere** and the plural definite article **le**.

> **Sono le** due.
> **Sone le** tre.
> **Sono le** quattro.

In official schedules, the 24-hour clock is preferred, as Italian time does not use A.M. or P.M. After 12 noon, add 12 to the P.M. hour for the 24-hour time.

To express minutes past the hour use **e** + the number of minutes.

> Sono le tre **e** venti.   *It is 3:20.*

To express less than 30 minutes before the hour, use **meno** + the number of minutes.

> Sono le quattro **meno** venti.   *It is twenty to four.*

For multiples of 15 minutes, one can use:

un quarto	*a quarter of an hour*
mezzo/a	*a half hour*
tre quarti	*three quarters of an hour*

The unit of a day can also be used to express certain times. The article is dropped and the singular verb is used.

È mezzogiorno.	*It is midday.*
È mezzanotte.	*It is midnight.*

When the prepositions **a** (*at*) or **da** (*from*) are used before times of the day, they combine with the definite article **l'** or **le**. (See contracted prepositions in Chapter 15.)

Remember, only **l'una** is feminine singular; the other hours are feminine plural, and therefore are preceded by the plural article **le** or its contraction.

> Ieri sera sono mi sono addormentata **all'1.00**, e oggi sono stanchissima!
> Generalmente Roberto lavora **dalle** 8.00 **alle** 13.00 e **dalle** 17.00 **alle** 19.00.

Proverbi con i numeri

Non **c'è** due senza tre.
There is no two without a three. (Things come in threes.)

Meglio **un uovo** oggi che **una gallina** domani.
Better one egg today than a chicken tomorrow.

ESERCIZIO
17·1

Determine the missing number in each sequence.

1. cinque   dieci   _____   venti

2. venti   quaranta   _____   ottanta

3. _____   diecimila   quindicimila   ventimila

4. mille   centomila   un milione   _____

To express dates, Italian uses the definite article **il** or **l'** + cardinal number + month + year.

Oggi è il 15 settembre, 2013.   *Today is September 15.*
L'8 marzo è la festa internazionale della donna.   *March 8 is International Women's Day.*

Attenzione!

Dates are written numerically as they are said. The fourth of July is 4/7, and Christmas is 25/12.

The first of the month is an ordinal number, and all the other dates are cardinal numbers.

il 1 gennaio → il **primo** gennaio
il 5 maggio → il cinque maggio

The year is written as it is in English but is never divided into hundreds and tens. 1954 is pronounced and written out as:

millenovecentocinquantaquattro, 2013 as duemilatredici

Filastrocca

This is a rhyme for learning the number of days in each month. **Aprile** has been shortened to **april**, and **hanno** has been shortened to **han** to accommodate the rhythm.

30 giorni ha novembre, con april, giugno e settembre. Di 28 ce n'è uno, tutti gli altri ne han 31.

ESERCIZIO
17·2

Read aloud the events and match them with the appropriate dates. You do not need to understand every word; let the proper names guide you.

1492   2002   1861   1517   2008   1776   1914

1. _____ Cristoforo Colombo sbarca a Guanahani, credendo di essere arrivato in India.

2. _____ Martin Lutero affigge le 95 tesi alla porta del Duomo di Wittenberg.

3. _____ Gli Stati Uniti dichiarano l'indipendenza dalla Gran Bretagna.

4. _____ Si proclama l'unità d'Italia.

5. _____ Inizia la prima guerra mondiale.

6. _____ L'euro è adottato come moneta europea.

7. _____ Gli Stati Uniti eleggono Barack Obama.

ESERCIZIO
17·3

Read and translate the dates of these historical events.

1. Roma è stata fondata il **21 aprile, 753** a.C.

_____

2. Giulio Cesare è stato assassinato il **15 marzo 44** a.C.

_____

3. La caduta dell'impero Romano è avvenuta nel **476.**

_____

4. Dante Alighieri è nato nel **1265.**

_____

5. La prima pila elettrica è stata costruita da Alessandro Volta nel **1880.**

_____

6. La caffettiera Moka Bialetti è stata inventata nel **1933.**

_____

ESERCIZIO

17·4

Write out the following sentences using numerals and the 24-hour clock.

1. Sono le due.

_____

2. È mezzanotte e venti.

_____

3. Sono le sei e quanrantacinque.

_____

4. Ho un appuntamento all'una e tre quarti.

_____

5. Generalmente cenano verso le otto.

_____

6. Non vado mai a dormire prima delle undici e mezza.

_____

7. Finisco di lavorare a mezzanotte meno un quarto.

_____

8. Devo uscire alle sei meno un quarto.

_____

9. Il treno parte alle nove e un quarto.

_____

10. Arriviamo a Napoli alle dieci e quaranta.

_____

Cognates and false friends

As you discover the many cognates that Italian and English share, you will have a great number of new words at your fingertips and will acquire a rich vocabulary in no time. There are, however, words similar in both languages that turn out to have no connection whatsoever. These words are commonly known as "false friends."

False friends and tricky translations

In the early 1900s, a wave of Italian immigrants came to the United States to work as stone masons and construction workers, and helped build hotels and apartment buildings in the big cities. Since then, countless tenants and patrons may have wondered why faucets marked with a C release hot water rather than cold. False friends are to blame: the Italian workers assumed that C stood for **caldo**, causing patrons and tenants to scald themselves in the bathtub. In this case, *cold* is the false friend of **caldo**, while *scald* is the cognate.

False friends are words that sound almost identical in two languages but have a completely different meaning. They may "deceive" us into thinking they are cognates, causing us to use them inaccurately. The reason for this comes from the fact that English derives from Latin and Greek (as Italian does) but also has many words with Germanic and Celtic roots, as in the word *kalt*, which means "cold." The similarity in sound between *kalt* and **caldo** is a coincidence and is an example of how false friends can create linguistic misunderstandings. Recognizing false cognates as you come across them and using them correctly several times in writing and speaking should gradually solve the problem.

The first column lists the most common Italian false friends with the correct English translation in the second column. In the third column, we have the English false friend with the the correct Italian translation in the fourth column. Similarly, each Italian word in the first column does not translate into the English word in the third column.

ITALIAN (F.F.)	ENGLISH MEANING	ENGLISH (F.F.)	ITALIAN MEANING
accidente	*negative event*	*accident*	incidente
argomento	*topic*	*argument*	discussione
camera	*room*	*camera*	macchina fotografica
conduttore	*train conductor*	*conductor*	direttore, maestro
conferenza	*lecture*	*conference*	convegno
confronto	*comparison*	*confrontation*	disputa, scontro
contesto	*context*	*contest*	gara
disgrazia	*misfortune*	*shame, disgrace*	vergogna
fattoria	*farm*	*factory*	fabbrica
lettura	*reading* (n)	*lecture*	conferenza
libreria	*bookstore, bookshelf*	*library*	biblioteca
romanzo	*novel*	*romance*	storia
sensibile	*sensitive*	*sensible, competent*	in gamba

The more problematic examples are those whose meanings may not be glaringly different and may therefore not readily be noticed by the learner. For example, **attualmente** means *currently, at the moment*. If someone is **sensitiva**, it means they are *psychic*. Telling someone you will go out **eventualmente** means that you will do so only as a *last resort*. **Parenti** are not *parents* but *relatives*, **delusione** means *disappointment*, and **confrontare** is *to compare*. **Lettura** means *reading (n)*, while **conferenza** means *lecture*. As learners recognize and take note of these false cognates in reading, speaking, and listening, these errors will gradually disappear.

There are a smaller number of Italian words that by coincidence are spelled exactly the same as English words but have different meanings. For example, **fame** = *hunger*, **cane** = *dog*, and **sale** = *salt* are just a few. But if you give the Italian words a closer look, you will see that they are related to the English words *famine, canine,* and *saline*.

Spelling tips

There are letters or groups of letters that are transcribed according to regular patterns. Being aware of these common patterns will help you learn to pronounce and spell these words correctly. The symbol → tells you how the English letters are generally transformed into Italian.

ENGLISH	→	ITALIAN			
ct	→	tt	dottore	attore	trattore
-ction, -ption	→	-zione	azione	dizionario	percezione
x	→	s	esempio	esperto	espressivo
-ble	→	-bile	probabile	possibile	incredibile
-nt	→	-nte	importante	differente	continente
-y	→	-ia or à	biologia	università	città
-nce	→	-nza	danza	importanza	confidenza
-ous	→	-oso	geloso	ansioso	ingegnoso

There are also some verbs whose meanings may not match exactly in the two languages and have slightly different meanings.

sapere (*to know how to, or know about something*)	**vs.**	**conoscere** (*to know someone or something*)
So nuotare.		**Conosci** Riccardo?
I know how to swim.		*Do you know Richard?*
Sai dove abita?		**Conosci** la storia italiana?
Do you know where he lives?		*Are you acquainted with Italian history?*

Notice also how **sapere** is rarely followed by an object noun, while **conoscere** is almost always followed by an object noun or a noun phrase.

andare (*to go*)	vs.	**venire** (*to come*)

Andate al cinema?
Are you going to the movies?

Venite a casa mia?
Are you coming to my place?

visitare (*to visit a place*)	vs.	**andare a trovare** (*to visit a person*)

Visitiamo il Grand Canyon?
Shall we visit the Grand Canyon?

Andiamo a trovare la nonna?
Shall we visit Grandma?

suonare (*to play an instrument*)	vs.	**giocare a** (*to play [a game or sport]*)

Suono il pianoforte.
I play the piano.

Gioco a calcio.
I play soccer.

potere (*to be able to, can or may*)	vs.	**riuscire a** (*to be able*)

Posso entrare?
May I come in?

Non **riesco a** vedere il prezzo.
I can't see the price.

Puoi chiamarmi domani?
Can you call me tomorrow?

Non **riesco a** capire.
I can't understand it.

soggetto (*grammatical subject*)	vs.	**materia** (*subject of study*)

Qual è il **soggetto** della frase?
What is the subject of the sentence?

Quale **materie** studi?
What subjects do you study?

ESERCIZIO
18·1

Correct the errors in the following sentences, and then translate them into English.

1. Maurizio gioca il pianoforte e la tromba.

_____

_____

2. Veniamo al cinema stasera?

_____

_____

3. È un bambino fragile e sensitivo.

_____

_____

4. Conosci se c'è una banca qui vicino?

_____

_____

5. Puoi comprare quel libro in biblioteca.

_____

_____

6. Isabella visita sua cugina l'anno prossimo.

_____

_____

7. Io e la mia sorella abbiamo avuto un argomento.

_____

_____

8. Davide suonava molto bene a tennis.

_____

_____

9. Sapete il ristorante dove andiamo stasera?

_____

_____

10. Su quella strada ci sono molti accidenti.

_____

_____

ESERCIZIO
18·2

Translate the following false friends into Italian and use them in a sentence.

1. *accident* _____

2. *subject* _____

3. *actually* _____

4. *to visit a person* _____

5. *to know (a person)* _____

6. *camera* _____

7. *eventually* _____

8. *novel* _____

9. *lecture* _____

10. *conference* _____

Translate the following sentences from English to Italian, being aware that they all contain at least one false friend.

1. What subjects are you studying this year?

   _____

2. The bookstore is in Piazza Argentina.

   _____

3. I am sensitive to the cold.

   _____

4. There is a conference on the euro crisis next week.

   _____

5. Eco's lecture was difficult for many of the students.

   _____

6. Does that conductor know how to play the piano?

   _____

7. We're visiting Isabella in Rome this summer.

   _____

8. The children are visiting a farm near Florence.

   _____

9. The old factory has been transformed into a museum.

   _____

10. I left my camera in my hotel room!

    _____

Answer key

1   Spelling and pronunciation

1·1   giusto, cento, calcio, giovane, ghiaccio, cena, Sicilia, giugno, c'è, laggiù

1·2

gn as in **prugna**	**sh** as in *sciarpa*	**sk** as in *scarpa*	**gl** as in **figlio**
giugno	prosciutto	sconto	miglio
sogno	scendere	bruschetta	luglio
montagna	sciare	ascoltare	aglio

1·3   1. perché   2. vendere   3. probabile   4. devono   5. amabile   6. città
       7. diciannovesimo   8. bellissimo   9. artistico   10. leggere

1·4   1. gondola   2. chiamano   3. però   4. impossibile   5. caffè   6. studiano
       7. preferiscono   8. Napoli   9. Taranto   10. Ligure

1·5   generale, giunto, sgelo, bacio, celeste

1·7   1. Dove abita tua sorella?
       2. La lezione è molto difficile.
       3. È probabile che arriverà tardi.
       4. Non è semplice arrivare in quella piazza.
       5. Preferisco il clima arido a quello piovoso.
       6. Cantano molto bene quei ragazzi.
       7. Se hai fame, guarda nel frigorifero.
       8. Per secondo prendo la sogliola ai ferri.
       9. Suo marito fa lo psicologo.
       10. I miei amici mi telefonano stasera.

1·8   1. abitano   2. esercitano   3. pagano   4. indicano   5. praticano   6. giocano
       7. predicano   8. prendono   9. leggono   10. evitano

1·9

Third-person verb	Ends in **-ile**	Ends in **-ogo, -olo/a, -omo, -ofo, -ero**	**-ere** infinitive	Ends in **-iaco**
telefonano	impossibile	cardiologo	ammettere	timido
devono	fossile	economo	dividere	allergico
abitano	portatile	filosofo	esprimere	antipatico
tornano	amabile	fiammifero	rispondere	austriaco
decidono	disabile	analogo	riconoscere	ipocondriaco

2   Nouns, gender, and number

2·1   1. il   2. la   3. lo   4. la   5. la   6. il   7. il   8. il   9. la   10. la

2·2

Masculine	Feminine
	signora
dottore	
	madre
professore	
	studentessa
scrittore	
	nipote
fratello	
	donna

2·3   1. la / c   2. il / e   3. la / f   4. il/la / d   5. il / h   6. la / i   7. l' / b   8. la / g   9. la / a   10. il / j

2·4   1. il nipote   2. lo scrittore   3. la presidente   4. il collega   5. la donna   6. il marito
7. il dottore   8. la dea   9. il genero   10. l'insegnante

2·5

Masculine singular	Masculine plural	Feminine singular	Feminine plural
stadio	stadi		
		università	università
sport	sport		
parco	parchi		
medico	medici		
		camicia	camicie
film	film		
		focaccia	focacce
zio	zii		
		tesi	tesi

3   Articles

3·1   1. uno stadio   2. un'insalata   3. uno psicologo   4. un'automobile   5. una città   6. una stazione
7. una mano   8. una serie   9. un albergo   10. un tedesco

3·2   1. la   2. X   3. le   4. gli   5. il   6. X   7. l'   8. le   9. le   10. X

3·3   1. lo, gli sport   2. l', le arie   3. la, le tesi   4. il, i film   5. la, le foto   6. l', le auto   7. l', le estati
8. il, i papà   9. lo, gli psichiatri or la, le psichiatre   10. la, le parentesi

4   Adjectives

4·1   1. libri gialli   2. studenti universitari   3. piazze romane   4. buone regole   5. sete leggere
6. vestiti chiari   7. pizzerie antiche   8. quadri famosi   9. care amiche   10. strade silenziose

4·2   1. ragazza intelligente   2. libro interessante   3. città affascinante   4. attrice francese
5. sport internazionale   6. domanda difficile   7. bambino vivace   8. vestito elegante
9. lezione importante   10. film francese

4·3   1. 4   2. 1   3. 2   4. 1   5. 2   6. 1   7. 3   8. 1   9. 2   10. 2

4·4   1. d   2. f   3. j   4. h   5. k   6. a   7. b   8. c   9. g   10. e

4·5   1. h   2. f   3. i   4. c   5. d   6. b   7. j   8. a   9. e   10. g

4·6   1. di   2. che   3. che   4. della   5. che   6. delle   7. degli   8. di   9. che   10. di

4·7   1. Mario è più simpatico di Giacomo.
2. Le montagne sono più alte delle colline.
3. Giovanna è tanto (così) studiosa quanto (come) sua sorella.
4. Quell'attore è più bello che intelligente.
5. L'autobus è tanto (così) veloce quanto (come) il tram.
6. Lo spagnolo è più facile del francese.
7. I cani sono più affettuosi dei pescirossi.
8. La Cina è meno grande della Russia.

9. Leggere *la Divina commedia* è più difficile che leggere *il Decameron.*

10. Kobe Bryant è più famoso di Vasco Rossi.

4·8
1. I cornetti in quel bar sono ottimi.
2. Roberto è il fratello minore.
3. Salieri fu un compositore minore.
4. Maradona è stato il calciatore migliore.
5. Abitano al piano superiore.
6. Quel film è di pessimo gusto.
7. Quell'avvocato ha una pessima reputazione.
8. Dante Alighieri è considerato il sommo/massimo poeta italiano.
9. Gli spaghetti alla carbonara sono ottimi!
10. L'Orvieto Classico è migliore del vino della casa.

4·9
1. La casa è grande.
2. Questo pacco è pesante.
3. Giovanni è un ragazzo dinamico.
4. Roberto è più magro di Antonio.
5. Questa strada è larga.
6. L'esame di chimica è facilissimo!
7. Nel negozio ho visto delle sedie moderne.
8. La mia bici è vecchissima.
9. Le mie amiche sono nervose (stressate).
10. Il giovane professore è bravissimo.

5 Adverbs

5·1
1. relativamente 2. brevemente 3. esattamente 4. veramente 5. semplicemente 6. possibilmente 7. raramente 8. francamente 9. direttamente 10. probabilmente

5·2
1. d / quando 2. e / ancora 3. a / perché 4. i / come 5. f / quanto 6. b / già 7. j / come 8. g / spesso 9. c / mai 10. h

5·3
1. Quando comincia l'inverno?
2. Com'è Claudia?
3. Quanto costava il pane?
4. Perché si arrabbia?
5. Quando torna?
6. Come vanno le lezioni?
7. Dove abitava?
8. Dove mette la macchina?

5·4
1. raramente
2. velocemente
3. sempre
4. piano
5. pochissimo
6. spesso
7. seriamente
8. divinamente

5·5
Answers may vary.
1. piano
2. mai
3. sfortunata
4. benissimo
5. dentro
6. tanto, molto
7. dopo
8. puntuale, in anticipo

6 Introduction to verb tenses

6·1
1. ci sono
2. C'è
3. è
4. C'è, c'è
5. C'è
6. sono, è, è
7. C'è
8. Ci sono

6·2
Answers may vary.
1. No, ha torto.
2. No, non hanno fretta.
3. No, abbiamo sete.
4. No, non ho paura.
5. No, ho sonno.
6. No, ha caldo.
7. No, ho freddo.
8. No, hanno poco da fare.

6·3
1. Ho fame!
2. Hai ragione.
3. Ha freddo.
4. Abbiamo fretta.
5. Ha 21 anni?
6. Non abbiamo sete.
7. Avete caldo?
8. Ha sonno.
9. Ho paura!
10. Hanno torto.

1. abbiamo sete
2. ho sonno
3. hanno fretta
4. hai torto

5. ha paura
6. ho fame
7. avete caldo
8. abbiamo freddo

7 Present and present perfect tenses

7·1

amare (*to love*)	vedere (*to see*)	offrire (*to offer*)	capire (*to understand*)
	vedo	offro	
ami		offri	capisci
ama	vede		capisce
amiamo	vediamo	offriamo	
amate		offrite	capite
	vedono	offrono	capiscono

7·2

andare		fare		avere	
	andiamo		facciamo	ho	
vai	andate	fai		hai	avete
va		fa	fanno		

essere		tenere		bere	
sono	siamo		teniamo	bevo	beviamo
sei		tieni	tenete		bevete
	sono	tiene	tengono	beve	

dire		uscire		venire	
dico	diciamo		usciamo		veniamo
	esci		vieni	venite
dice	dicono	esce	escono	viene	

7·3

Answers will vary.
1. Anna va . . .
2. Gli italiani sono . . .
3. Io bevo . . .
4. Rob e Cecilia vengono . . .

5. Tu e Marco rimanete . . .
6. Io e Susanna veniamo . . .
7. Lei, signora Rossellini, esce . . .
8. Tu, Maria, fai . . .

7·4

1. Oggi parlo con il professore.
2. Oggi telefono alla zia.
3. Oggi capisco la lezione.
4. Oggi vendo qualcosa su eBay.
5. Oggi ho freddo.
6. Oggi guardo la TV.
7. Oggi ascolto la radio.
8. Oggi finisco la lezione.
9. Oggi ballo il tango.
10. Oggi preferisco il cappuccino.

Anche ieri ho parlato con il professore.
Anche ieri ho telefonato alla zia.
Anche ieri ho capito la lezione.
Anche ieri ho venduto qualcosa su eBay.
Anche ieri ho avuto freddo.
Anche ieri ho guardato la TV.
Anche ieri ho ascoltato la radio.
Anche ieri ho finito la lezione.
Anche ieri ho ballato il tango.
Anche ieri ho preferito il cappuccino.

7·5

1. Oggi Antonio torna tardi.
2. Oggi Amelia si sveglia presto.
3. Oggi tu e Amedeo partite per Napoli.
4. Oggi Paola e Franca vanno a scuola.
5. Oggi voi uscite alle 7.30.
6. Oggi io e i miei amici andiamo al cinema.
7. Oggi i ragazzi restano a casa.
8. Oggi Paola passa a casa mia.
9. Oggi Guglielmo non torna a New York.
10. Oggi Regina parte con Sandro.

Anche ieri è tornato tardi.
Anche ieri Amelia si è svegliata presto.
Anche ieri siete partiti per Napoli.
Anche ieri sono andate a scuola.
Anche ieri siete usciti alle 7.30.
Anche ieri siamo andati al cinema.
Anche ieri i ragazzi sono restati a casa.
Anche ieri è passata a casa mia.
Anche ieri non è tornato a New York.
Anche ieri è partita con Sandro.

7·6

1. Anna è dovuta andare a New York.
2. Hai potuto telefonare a Marco?

3. Amelia è voluta venire a casa.
4. I ragazzi sono potuti tornare.

	5. Ho dovuto lavorare fino a tardi.	7. Non sono potuto/a venire a cena.
	6. Sono voluti andare al mare.	8. Tu e Anna avete dovuto leggere questo libro.

7·7
1. L'opera è finita tardi.
2. Maria ha cominciato il lavoro.
3. La situazione è cambiata.
4. Marco è passato davanti a casa mia.
5. Lucia e Bob sono ritornati sabato.
6. Ho riportato il libro in biblioteca.
7. Il tempo è cambiato in autunno.
8. La musica è finita.
9. Il presidente ha cominciato il suo discorso.
10. Abbiamo passato l'estate in Italia.

7·8 *Answers will vary.*

8 Imperfect and past perfect tenses

8·1
1. dicevamo
2. bevevate
3. facevano
4. eri
5. facevo
6. prendeva
7. venivi
8. c'era
9. andavamo
10. erano

8·2
1. ero
2. abbiamo avuto
3. Faceva
4. andava
5. ho visto
6. sembrava
7. ha fatto
8. diceva, pensava

8·3
1. erano partiti
2. avevate mangiato
3. era ritornato/a
4. eri stato/a
5. era andato/a
6. avevate preso
7. aveva detto
8. avevamo chiesto
9. avevano messo
10. avevo studiato

9 Past absolute tense

9·1 Venni, vidi, vinsi.

9·2
1. scrisse, scrivere
2. compose, comporre
3. dipinse, dipingere
4. si trasferirono, trasferirsi
5. morì, morire
6. fece, fare
7. vinse, vincere
8. visse, vivere
9. si conobbero, conoscersi
10. si sposò, sposarsi

10 Future and future perfect tenses

10·1
1. parlerà
2. prenderanno
3. capirete
4. arriverò
5. leggeremo
6. pagherà
7. mangerete
8. metterò
9. arriveremo
10. dormiranno

10·2
1. Lavorerò domani.
2. Quando arriverà l'inverno, andremo in Sicilia.
3. Domani comincerà la scuola.
4. Tu e Giovanni tornerete l'anno prossimo?
5. Stasera resterò a casa.
6. La settimana prossima arriverà mia sorella!
7. Non vorrà andare al concerto.
8. Sarai qui per la festa?
9. Cosa farà quando finisce l'università?
10. Dovrò trovare un lavoro.

10·3
1. Maria sarà felice con il nuovo lavoro.
2. Avrai conosciuto molta gente interessante.
3. Avrò lasciato il mio libro sul treno.
4. Lo studente avrà perso l'autobus.

5. Avremo visto cento film!
6. La squadra italiana avrà vinto la partita.
7. Avrà molte domande.
8. Tornerà entro le 8.00.
9. Quanto avrò dormito?
10. Quanto costerà?

11   Present and perfect conditional tenses

11·1
1. Vorrei un bicchiere di acqua minerale, per favore.
2. Andrebbe a studiare.
3. Andremmo in Francia.
4. Sarebbe facile.
5. Vorremmo andare in vacanza.
6. Saranno contenti.
7. Partireste subito?
8. Andresti in Canada?
9. Non farei niente.
10. Quando torneresti?

11·2
1. f   2. g   3. h   4. i   5. e   6. d   7. c   8. b   9. a

11·3
1. studierebbe   5. cambierebbero
2. vorrei   6. dovresti
3. farebbe   7. avrebbe
4. andrei   8. sareste

11·4
1. Mi daresti una mano?
2. Mi farebbe lo sconto, signora?
3. Dottore, mi darebbe un appuntamento per domani?
4. Signori, potrebbero tornare domani?
5. Marco, potresti chiamarmi domani?
6. Verresti con me in Italia?
7. Professore, sarebbe possibile rimandare l'esame fino a domani?
8. Potrebbe ripetere la domanda, per favore?

12   The subjunctive

12·1
1. parli
   I believe that Mara speaks French.
2. insegni
   I think that Letizia teaches English.
3. chieda
   I doubt that Eleonora will apologize to me.
4. dica
   It isn't possible that you always tell lies!
5. guadagni
   Even though Maria earns a lot, she is always without money.
6. chiami
   I believe that student is named Andrea.
7. veda
   I think that Gaia and Jim see many French films.
8. decida
   I want to talk to you before you decide to quit your job.
9. parli
   It seems that Sandro often speaks of you.
10. paghi
   I don't want you to pay all the time!

12·2	assere	avere	parlare	prendere	finire
	sia	abbia	parli	prenda	**finisca**
	siamo	**abbiamo**	parliamo	prendiamo	finiamo
	siate	abbiate	**parliate**	prendiate	finiate
	siano	abbiano	parlino	**prendano**	finiscano

12·3
1. fosse venuto
2. sei partito
3. vince
4. vincessero
5. parte

6. dicessero
7. siano andati
8. fosse
9. piova
10. avessi

13 The imperative

13·1
1. invitarlo
2. Prepara
3. Invita
4. Mettiti

5. Digli
6. Falli
7. falla
8. beviamolo

13·2
1. Prenda
2. Compri
3. Non torni
4. Salutate, Salutino
5. Non si preoccupi

6. Faccia
7. Entri
8. Torni
9. Si accomodi
10. Si calmi

13·3
1. Facciamo una festa!
2. Non mangiare tutta la pizza!
3. Torna!
4. Studiamo insieme!
5. Chiama tua madre!

6. Chiudi la porta!
7. Apri la finestra!
8. Stai attento/a!
9. Non fare tardi!
10. Scrivi presto!

13·4
1. Parli più lentamente, per favore.
2. Ripeta la domanda, per favore.
3. Mi dia ancora due giorni, per favore.
4. Abbia pazienza, per favore!
5. Non si arrabbi, per favore.
6. Parli più forte, per favore.
7. Apra la finestra, per favore.
8. Ci mostri quel film, per favore.
9. Non fumi in classe, per favore!
10. Risponda ai nostri messaggi, per favore!

14 The passive voice

14·1
1. Il concorso è stato vinto dal baritono americano.
2. L'*Isola di Arturo* è stato scritto da Elsa Morante.
3. Quel film sarà stato girato a Cinecittà.
4. La partita sarà stata vinta dalla squadra del Cameroon.
5. Il vino rosso sarà portato da Marco e Paola.
6. I fiori sono stati piantati da Roberto.
7. Le nuove leggi saranno approvate dal governo.
8. I temi in italiano erano (venivano) corretti da quel professore.
9. La torta sarà stata mangiata dai ragazzi.
10. L'aria di *Aida* è stata cantata dal soprano.

14·2
1. Si è preparata la cena.
2. Si pulirà la camera.
3. Si è accettata l'offerta.
4. Si è restaurata la casa.
5. Si consiglia quel libro.
6. Si accettano carte di credito.

7. Si sono venduti i quadri di Warhol.

8. Non si sono mai pubblicate le sue opere.

9. Non si vende la mozzarella buona al supermercato.

10. Si sono scelti i suoi documentari.

14·3
1. Si beve troppo la sera.
2. Si guadagna poco da McDonald's.
3. Si parla italiano in questo negozio?
4. Non si fa così.
5. Si vive bene in Italia?
6. Si viaggia bene in treno?
7. Oggi si entra gratis alla Galleria Borghese.
8. Dalla finestra si vedeva il mare.

14·4 1. I   2. I   3. P   4. I   5. I   6. P   7. I   8. I

14·5
1. Si è partiti alle 10.00.
2. Si è trovato il gatto.
3. Ci si è svegliati tardi stamattina.
4. Si è fatta la vendemmia in ottobre?
5. Si è tornati dalla Sardegna in luglio.
6. Non si è mangiata l'insalata come antipasto.
7. Si sono viste più stelle nel deserto?
8. Si è arrivati presto in metropolitana.

15 Prepositions

15·1   1. e   2. d   3. f   4. c   5. b   6. g   7. a   8. j   9. h   10. i

15·2
1. a, in   6. a, a
2. in, in   7. a, in, per
3. di, a, con   8. da, a
4. da, da, in   9. tra / fra
5. in, Per   10. a

15·3
1. alla   5. dal
2. sul   6. nel
3. alle   7. sui
4. dalle, alle   8. allo

15·4   1. a   2. alla   3. al, a   4. a, a   5. in   6. a   7. in, da   8. in, dalla, alla

15·5   *Answers may vary.*
1. Vado in bici.
2. Di solito mangio presto.
3. Abito a Roma.
4. Andiamo da Silvio.
5. Vado a piedi.
6. Sono le otto di mattina.
7. Ho molto da fare.
8. In realtà preferisco l'acqua frizzante.
9. Di niente!
10. Da piccolo era biondissimo.

15·6
1. Abito a Roma, e vado a lavoro in metropolitana.
   I live in Rome, and I go to work by subway.
2. Studia quasi sempre in salotto.
   She/He always studies in the living room.
3. Sei tornata a casa tardi?
   Did you (f.) get home late?
4. Stasera andiamo a teatro.
   Tonight we are going to the theater.
5. Parto da Roma in aereo.
   I'm leaving Rome by plane.